info@kinfolkmag.com
www.kinfolkmag.com

Printed in the United States of America

Publication Design by Amanda Jane Jones
Cover photograph by Tec Petaja
Cover Stylist Nathan Williams

weldon**owen**

415 Jackson Street, Suite 200,
San Francisco, CA 94111
Telephone: 415 291 0100
Fax: 415 291 8841
www.wopublishing.com

Weldon Owen is a division of

BONNIER

KINFOLK

SUBSCRIBE

VISIT SHOP.KINFOLKMAG.COM

FOUR VOLUMES EACH YEAR

CONTACT US

If you have any questions or comments,
email us at *info@kinfolkmag.com*

SUBSCRIPTIONS

For questions regarding your subscription,
email us at *subscribe@kinfolkmag.com*

STOCKISTS

If you would like to carry *Kinfolk*,
email us at *distribution@kinfolkmag.com*

SUBMISSIONS

Send all submissions to
submissions@kinfolkmag.com

WWW.KINFOLKMAG.COM

WELCOME

*We don't all observe the same traditions, enjoy the same dishes,
or even call these winter holidays by the same names, but surely we share
an appreciation of how these months pull us together.*

I don't have children, but when that day comes, I'm determined to plan the month of December with every holiday tradition in the book. I'll spare them only the worst (caroling and gag gifts), and draw up a timetable with the others for a rigorous regimen of holiday cheer. I say this now with a straight face, but realize that my enthusiasm will wane after cleaning the first mess of tinsel. It seems like traditions naturally come with the season—sugar cookies, *The Nutcracker*, sledding—but there's always someone stepping up to make them happen. This issue is our "thanks" to whoever has been behind these activities for us. We're looking back with gratitude and looking forward with ideas to try out this year like simmer pots (p. 85), tree hunting (p. 80), proper fire-building techniques (p. 60), and pine-needle teas (p. 82).

Rebecca Parker Payne captures the theme of this issue perfectly in her essay "Making a Tribe" (p. 41) with a nostalgic tribute to her parents, followed by a challenge to maintain winter traditions for ourselves. "We are adults, and we are, in our best selves, independent, vibrant, thriving, and capable," she says, "...we can take the traditions into our homes, draw them through the sieve of our personalities, sprinkle them with whimsy, mold them to our own relationships. In doing so, we hold a respectful ownership of the season, where it cannot exist outside of us." So there's the challenge: step up, (wo)man up, and make time for a gingerbread house. Someone mastered that arduous tradition for us (the humiliation of caroling, soggy tobogganing, wrapping gifts at miserable hours of the night), and now it's our turn to embrace the epic fails (note to avoid Christmas in a Box and flashy frozen-food catalogues, p. 114) and the tried-and-true wins (Spiced Figs Cranberry Sauce, p. 30).

We don't all observe the same traditions, enjoy the same dishes, or even call these winter holidays by the same names, but surely we share an appreciation of how these months pull us together. Cheers to that.

NATHAN WILLIAMS, EDITOR OF KINFOLK MAGAZINE

NATHAN WILLIAMS
Editor
Portland, Oregon

AMANDA JANE JONES
Designer
Ann Arbor, Michigan

DOUG BISCHOFF
Sales & Distribution
Portland, Oregon

JULIE POINTER
Features Editor & Gatherings
Portland, Oregon

KATIE SEARLE-WILLIAMS
Features Editor
Portland, Oregon

NATASHA MEAD
Design Assistant
New Zealand

ERICA MIDKIFF
Copy Editor
Birmingham, Alabama

PAIGE BISCHOFF
Accountant
Portland, Oregon

ANDREW GALLO
Film Maker
Portland, Oregon

KATIE STRATTON
Painter
Dayton, Ohio

NICOLE FRANZEN
Photographer
Brooklyn, New York

AMY MERRICK
Florist & Writer
Brooklyn, New York

PARKER FITZGERALD
Photographer
Portland, Oregon

NIKAELA MARIE PETERS
Writer
Winnipeg, Canada

JESSICA COMINGORE
Online Editor
Los Angeles, California

KATHRIN KOSCHITZKI
Photographer
Munich, Germany

ALPHA SMOOT
Photographer
New York City, New York

NICO ALARY
Photographer & Writer
Victoria, Australia

GENTL & HYERS
Photographers
New York, New York

AUSTIN SAILSBURY
Writer
Copenhagen, Denmark

LISA MOIR
Stylist
San Francisco, California

LEO PATRONE
Photographer
Salt Lake City, Utah

TEC PETAJA
Photographer
Nashville, Tennessee

CARISSA GALLO
Photographer
Portland, Oregon

MICHAEL MULLER
Photographer
Austin, Texas

JOY KIM
Illustrator
Portland, Oregon

RICHARD ASLAN
Writer
Bristol, United Kingdom

SAER RICHARDS
Writer
Brooklyn, New York

MEGAN MARTIN
Writer
Palm Beach, Florida

SARAH SUKSIRI
Writer
Indianapolis, Indiana

THE JEWELS OF NEW YORK
Food Stylists
New York, New York

JOHN TROXEL
Photographer
Chicago, Illinois

LAURIE FRANKEL
Photographer
San Francisco, California

TRAVIS ROGERS
Writer
Paris, France

LAURA DART
Photographer
Portland, Oregon

PETRINA TINSLAY
Photographer
Sydney, Australia

YOUNG & HUNGRY
Photographers
Los Angeles, California

OLIVIA RAE JAMES
Writer & Photographer
Charleston, South Carolina

ELODIE RAMBAUD
Stylist
Paris, France

JULIA MANCHIK
Illustrator
Auburn, Washington

RYAN ROBERT MILLER
Photographer
Los Angeles, California

ANNE STARK DITMEYER
Writer
Paris, France

MELISA MICHELE SIBLEY
Stylist
Portland, Oregon

NICHOLAS PARKER
Writer
Albuquerque, New Mexico

YOLANDA DE MONTIJO
Writer
Glen Ellen, California

LISA WARNINGER
Photographer
Portland, Oregon

ADAM JONES
Photographer
Brooklyn, New York

REBECCA PARKER PAYNE
Writer
Richmond, Virginia

CHELSEA FUSS
Stylist
Portland, Oregon

RACHEL BROWN
Photographer & Writer
Brooklyn, New York

MARK WEINBERG
Photographer
New York City, New York

ERIN BOYLE
Writer
Brooklyn, New York

EMMA ROBERTSON
Stylist & Knitter
Los Angeles, California

DANICA VAN DE VELDE
Writer
Perth, Australia

DAVID WINWARD
Writer
Salt Lake City, Utah

EVAN HANLON
Writer
Brooklyn, New York

SCOTT ANDERSON
Writer
Orange County, California

LOUISA THOMSEN BRITS
Writer
East Sussex, United Kingdom

ROSA PARK
Photographer & Writer
Bath, United Kingdom

MARK W. FREE
Barista
Melbourne, Australia

ONE

TWO

1 WELCOME

2 KINFOLK COMMUNITY

8 FINDING QUIET IN THE JUNGLE URBANUS
Saer Richards

14 THE PERFECT CUP: MARK FREE
Nico Alary

17 AEROPRESS RECIPE
Mark W. Free

18 A WAYFARER'S SERIES: THE RIVER WYE
Austin Sailsbury

25 CRANBERRIES: BUSH TO BOWL
Parker Fitzgerald & Danica van de Velde

30 SPICED FIGS CRANBERRY SAUCE
The Jewels of New York

34 PIERRE JANCOU, CHEF AT VIVANT PARIS
Anne Stark Ditmeyer

37 HOW TO BE NEIGHBORLY: GIFT GIVING
Julie Pointer

41 MAKING A TRIBE
Rebecca Parker Payne

50 BUCHTELN: A FAMILY RECIPE
Kathrin Koschitzki

57 EVERYDAY SILVER
Nicholas Parker

58 MORSELS WE KEEP AFTER THE MEAL
Erin Boyle

60 TO BUILD A FIRE
David Winward

67 THE BAKER BROTHERS
Rosa Park

FEW

73 OUR TREE: THE GRACEFUL EVERGREEN
Louisa Thomsen Brits

80 EVERGREEN FORAGING GUIDE
Joy Kim

82 HOME USES FOR THE EVERGREEN TREE
Megan Martin

85 SIMMER POTS
Katie Searle-Williams

86 STAFF LUNCHES WITH THE MAST BROTHERS
Julie Pointer

90 WINTER WEEKENDS
Yolanda de Montijo

97 SYNCHRONICITY
Olivia Rae James

98 EATING REVERENTLY
Nikaela Marie Peters

100 HOLIDAY HEALTH RULES
Travis Rogers

102 SHEEP TO SHAWL
Young & Hungry

109 INTERVIEW: ANY STYLE CATERING
Jessica Comingore

110 HOLIDAY VIGNETTES
John Troxel

114 GREAT AUNT BETTY'S BREAD SAUCE
Richard Aslan

117 A BRIEF HISTORY OF BREAKFAST
Sarah Suksiri

118 BROOKLYN STOOP
Rachel Brown

121 LOOSE-LEAF BOOKENDS
Scott Anderson

122 BUVETTE: REFRESHMENTS
Evan Hanlon

128 MY WINTER GARDEN
Amy Merrick & Parker Fitzgerald

136 CREDITS

137 KEEP IN TOUCH

ONE

ENTERTAINING FOR ONE

○

FINDING QUIET IN THE JUNGLE URBANUS

The untameable city is occasionally, briefly quieted.

WORDS BY SAER RICHARDS & PHOTOGRAPHS BY NICOLE FRANZEN

The sheer volume of people living in such close proximity is often the source of friction. In the hot heat season, tempers rise and patience wanes. Colder times bury everyone under layers of flannel, which stymies the barely existent desire to interact.

The city is a voracious beast; it consumes many a man. Unforgiving, it reserves the ability to tame it for the resolutely brave or flawlessly stupid. Maybe they are one and the same.

It bucks and charges during the day while throngs of multi-colored peoples on foot and in cars ripple uniformly through its streets, like specks navigating a wild creature's back. They are connected in an organic way, yet remain as separate from each other as one hair shaft is from the next.

It has been said that living in a city hardens a person, takes away that element of their being that makes them empathically human. It certainly does something. But that should be expected when in the presence of an entity wild.

The particular characteristics of the city can make it feel utterly foreign to those that have never lived in one. Graffiti is splashed across surfaces, marking the fabric of the terrain. Street fashion runs the gamut of conventional to *avant-garde*. Buskers play homemade tunes on instruments from lands far and near, singing songs of love and fear, joy and pain. Buildings are unusually tall. They stretch into the sky, tops tapering off into the fog of low-lying clouds. Their magnitude makes them otherworldly, not least because they have touched the sky.

The city soundtrack plays on repeat: Car horns honk. Bike messenger brakes screech. Manhole covers hiss with dubious steam. Sirens blare at almost every street corner. People loudly talk, laugh, and yell into mobile phones. And deep, deep down, the city rumbles.

It is no wonder that most walk around plugged in. White ear-buds and strings are a giveaway that they are listening to music or talking on the phone; some have glazed eyes, absorbed in audio books. Much about the city encourages separation; it's a wonder anyone can connect.

Being carried on the back of this beast leaves inhabitants emotionally and physically scuffed. The sheer volume of people living in such close proximity is often the source of friction. In the hot heat season, tempers rise and patience wanes. Colder times bury everyone under layers of flannel, which stymies the barely existent desire to interact.

The fear to speak to each other exists as a method of self-preservation. Everyone is striving for the same goal—mastery over this creature they ride each day. Scared to reveal their strategy to the next man, they eye each other suspiciously, like prisoners privy to the answer in a quest for liberation.

This seemingly harsh exterior hides the person within, stifles the unmistakable empathic instinct to nurture, share, and commune.

And yet we do.

Occasionally, just sometimes.

A friend of mine traveled to Sicily for a holiday with friends. They found a café, old and beautiful, off the beaten path. "What could be more memorable than coffee in Sicily?" she asked. They entered the establishment and requested a cup each, to go. The proprietor gestured for them to sit. "To go" was a foreign concept there. What rush could there possibly be

City landscapes are deceptive. At the seams are glimmers of nature;
its dwellers enforce a peace in their lives by seeking out these crevices to create
warm and most welcoming moments.

that would deny one the pleasure of pausing to savour a cup of coffee? Until denied the option of walking with her drink, she'd never realized how city living had made her accustomed to the mobility of her meals.

I was born in a large city on one continent and currently live in a big city on another; this brings specific ignorances. Especially when it comes to perceiving how nature and landscape in areas less populous behave. Learning that night stars routinely cover the skies like glitter on a dark velvet quilt, or that the moon can light a path with a glow similar to that of a neon bulb, was surprising. These things seemed too fantastical to be true. But they're real. I saw them. Once.

The city has its own night. Identified mostly by the fact that its pace alters. Swarming cars outnumber people two to one; headlights emit a brilliance that creates a feigned daylight. They illuminate streets and the sky, obscuring the heavenly luminaries in a fluorescent fog of tungsten. If by day the creature bucks, at night it certainly heaves.

But no matter how wild a beast, all creatures have to take rest; to retreat and seek calm.

City landscapes are deceptive. At the seams are glimmers of nature; its dwellers enforce a peace in their lives by seeking out these crevices to create warm and most welcoming moments.

I shall never forget the first time I dined on a residential rooftop in the heart of New York. In almost any other setting, such a notion would seem simply absurd at best: food, candles, blankets, tables—carefully carried onto a roof. But we wanted to collectively take respite from the beast. We sat on top of the city. Evaluating its landscape of ever-present lights—our equivalent of the stars on a clear country night. The usual noises tapered off as the beast's rumble seemingly calmed. We didn't notice what was going on underneath, only the conversation among us. We told stories by candlelight that flickered like campfire; no one noticed when they extinguished and left us in darkness.

It is the retreats of rooftops, speakeasies, basement cafés, and small apartment gardens that force the beast to become tranquil. These spaces are familiar in some other terrains, but unique in the context of a big city. For us they are our sanctuaries. The places where we can hear each other over the roar, and allow the energy around us to recede. We are allowed to be empathetic here—to share and commune before donning our coats and stepping back into the tumult that requires a force field of defensiveness for survival's sake.

These moments are a cure for the common way of life.

We don't have the forests and brooks that are home to the sound of birds chirping and the rush of water bubbling. We don't need to. We have our unique retreat, in ways only a city dweller can. Ours is an untamed city that we know how to lull to sleep. ○

THE PERFECT CUP: MARK FREE

*The perfect cup is not only about how you make it, or which bean you use,
but also (and just as importantly) who has made it for you.*

When asked to do a series about the perfect cup of coffee, the first person that came to mind was Mark Free. Mark is curator of the Black Coffee Pop-Up in Melbourne and manages Brother Baba Budan, one of the best cafés in the city. When I arrive at Mark's studio it's about 9 a.m., and despite the fact that it's the middle of summer, the sky is overcast and the day cool, and I'm glad I'm wearing a couple of layers. Perfect weather for drinking some coffee. His girlfriend Amy is there too, flipping through an old copy of *Crime and Punishment*.

Mark turns on the hot plates, weighs out the coffee, rinses the paper filter, and starts grinding the beans—medium-fine for the AeroPress. As he is carefully making a cup for each of us, I start shooting, and we casually talk about the perfect cup. Which origin? What time of day? Mark likes his around 10 a.m. Wake up, settle in, and then make the first AeroPress of the day. I'm loving how simple the method is. The grounds goes in the chamber, hot water is poured on top, and one minute later the AeroPress is flipped over a cup, and the now-brewed coffee is forced through the paper filter in about twenty seconds.

He tells me that coffee tastes better when you make it yourself, or when it is made by someone you know. The perfect cup is not only about how you make it, or which bean you use, but also (and just as importantly) who has made it for you. The first couple of cups are ready and the room fills with the aroma of freshly brewed coffee. My cup is perfectly exctracted, sweet and clean with complexity. Peach, apricot, and shortbread-biscuit flavors come to mind. It looks like it's going to rain. I put the camera down for a few minutes and we all quietly sip the warm beverage, looking out at the unsure weather. I'm thinking that this could be it, the perfect cup. A comfy couch, some single-origin beans, and a carefully prepared cup of coffee, made by a friend.

A BREWING SERIES BY NICO ALARY

AEROPRESS

INGREDIENTS	METHOD

INGREDIENTS

7 ounces water,
just shy of boiling

2 tablespoons coffee,
ground medium to fine,
like coarse beach sand

METHOD

This makes coffee for one or to share.

Grind your coffee fresh, if possible.

Fully extend the AeroPress chamber and plunger components and place inverted on the bench or scales with the filter cap off.

Preheat the AeroPress chamber with hot water and then discard.

Rinse the paper filter disk in the filter cap.

Add coffee grounds and boiled water to the chamber, ensuring all the grounds are saturated, and screw on the filter cap.

After 30 seconds, place your cup or decanter over the filter cap and carefully flip the AeroPress and cup.

Wait a further 30 seconds, then plunge for 20 seconds, stopping as soon as all the liquid is extracted and the press begins to gurgle—squeezing the grounds at the bottom of the press may lead to unpleasant, over-extracted flavors.

Recipe by Mark W. Free

A WAYFARER'S SERIES: THE RIVER WYE

*It was a Christmas unlike any other I had experienced before or since—
in a snowy English hollow with strangers who became friends, in a house where
sailboats are made, near a river called Wye.*

A WORK OF FICTION BY AUSTIN SAILSBURY

PHOTOGRAPHS BY NICOLE FRANZEN & PARKER FITZGERALD

By the afternoon of the day before Christmas Eve, I had resigned myself to my fate—I would be spending the most nostalgic, tradition-soaked, and easily enjoyable day of my year alone, in a deserted flat in soggy central England. Sure, there would be plenty of "Merry Christmas" phone calls and promises of presents in the mail, but it wouldn't be Mom and Dad, and there wouldn't be comfort food, and it wouldn't be home, so it wouldn't *really* be Christmas. But who could I blame? I was the one that had chosen to move halfway around the world—I was the one who had gone looking for adventure.

It was into the dark of evening and I was brewing a pot of tea when the buzzer rang, "Hullo, it's Lucy, can I come up?" Surprised but delighted to hear her bright voice, I buzzed her in and waited in the doorway as she hopped and clopped her jolly self all the way to the fourth floor. Little did I know, as Lucy made her way up the stairs, that she brought with her tidings of great joy—and an invitation to escape the solitude of an extraordinarily lonely holiday. Catching her breath on the landing, she started right into it, "So, I have an idea..."

It was early and wet and cold when we caught the train going west out of Birmingham. On board, the train cars were packed full of holiday travelers all a fuss with coats and children and promising packages. But despite the falling rain and frantic bustle of traffic, there was the overwhelming spirit of red-cheeked goodwill that you'd expect on Christmas Eve; people talked to one another freely across the aisles, old men sipped from shiny morning flasks, and somewhere on board a child was finding much joy in shaking a tiny sleigh bell. And as if on cue, when the train crawled out from under the protection of the station, the sky began to spit a small measure of floating white snow. Within a few minutes the grey and graffiti of the city dissolved into the eternal rolling greens of England, dusted with snow and spotted with sheep. As we traveled, Lucy reassured me that I was more than welcome, and that her parents were really happy that I had agreed to come—it was not an imposition.

When we arrived in Hereford, on the River Wye, it was midday and the town was a vision so idyllic it seemed artificial: the falling snow, last-minute shoppers popping in and out of golden-lit storefronts, twinkling lights strung overhead, and the philanthropic carolers on every other street corner. It was the chime of the cathedral bells and Lucy's urging that pulled me from my reverie, "Come on, we better move on before it starts getting dark." And so on we moved, first by bus toward the village where Lucy's parents lived, and then by foot, until a red car pulled over and offered to save us from the weather. Lucy saw my trepidation, "It's fine; around here, everyone gets rides to and from the bus stop—really."

It was fine after all, and the red car and driver deposited us safely at our destination as we exchanged thanks and well wishes. Then, with our bags in hand and snow collecting on our coats, we stood in front of Lucy's home—a historic red-bricked place with woods at the back and pasture to both sides. Woodsmoke trickled up from the chimneys and mixed together with that good, strong farm smell until the air was a kind of sensory carnival best experienced with closed eyes. Despite the cold, Lucy kindly let me soak it in a moment. When the door opened a woman appeared. She smiled at us smiling at her home and motioned us in.

The interior of the old house was rich with texture and history: stone floors worn smooth, thick plastered walls, irregular glass windowpanes, a spiral staircase, and a living room with every wall wrapped in floor-to-ceiling bookshelves—a storybook cottage filled with a thousand storybooks.

In the corner, beneath *The Complete Volumes of Dickens*, *The Arabian Nights*, and a well-worn set of *Encyclopedia Britannica*, stood an ancient but proud upright piano.

Lucy had told me that her mother was a musician in a symphony, as well as the village music teacher. She was tall with dark hair, and made us tea, asking about the train ride. When she sat down with us at the wooden table, she held Lucy's hand. Lucy's father emerged from his workshop, a thin man with a gray beard speckled with sawdust, and offered me a sturdy, weathered handshake. Lucy had told me that he, too, was a concert musician, but that during the winter months he built sailboats in his workshop—one sailboat every year from scratch. Her father also asked us about the train and then said, "Give me a few more minutes in the shop and then let's get busy bringing Christmas to life, okay?" We agreed, naturally, though I wasn't exactly sure what I was agreeing to.

As it turned out, "bringing Christmas to life" involved chopping down and carrying a small Christmas tree into the house from the woods outside, decorating the tree, stepping over the cat, distributing and lighting dozens of candles, preparing a pot of mulled wine, putting the turkey into the oven, hanging greenery over doorways, shooing the cat from the kitchen, cutting extra firewood, basting the turkey, tasting the mulled wine, setting out the violin and cello, stoking the fire, another glass of the wine, shooing the cat from the library, wrapping some small gifts, dressing the turkey, dressing the table, and dressing for dinner.

When all the candles were lit, with dinner revealed and the cat put away, we gathered around the table. We took a moment to absorb the glow of it all: the crumbling fire in the library, the simmer of the warm wine, and the heavy silence of the snow falling outside the windows. Another pause... another Christmas reverie. Then, with a cheerful but understated flourish, Lucy's father declared, "Well then, Christmas has come to life! Shall we celebrate?"

After dinner there was coffee and music—strings played by the professionals and the piano played by Lucy. Into the wee hours the family band made music as they had done every Christmas Eve, with a sold-out crowd of books, and the Ghost of Christmas Present conducting. Even I was roped into singing what I knew of the songs they chose. Before succumbing to sleep (and making way for St. Nicholas), we entertained one final family ritual: listening to Dylan Thomas read *A Child's Christmas in Wales*. Both women wrapped themselves in blankets and smiled as the confident voice of the poet spoke to us from an antique stereo. We listened enraptured until, with the last turn of the vinyl, the fire collapsed, the candles expired, and our small party went to our beds happy that Christmas morning was close at hand. That night, under patchwork quilts and a low roof, I dreamed of St. Nicholas sailing toward us on the River Wye, and I slept as peacefully as I can ever remember.

Christmas day came with sun and a snowy landscape, small gifts handed out, more songs on the violin, warm bread pudding, a walk in the snowy woods, and an afternoon reading of *The Cricket on the Hearth*. It was a Christmas unlike any other I had experienced before or since—in a snowy English hollow with strangers who became friends, in a house where sailboats are made, near a river called Wye. All because of of the kindness of a friend who believed Christmas was more than an event on the calendar but, rather, that Christmas is the bringing to life of the spirits that are best in humanity: hospitality and gratitude and friendship.

The wayfarer is by definition a leaver—one who leaves, goes, sets out into the world in order to find something. Leaving, of course, requires the risk of losing things, but it also opens the possibility of finding oneself as a character in a real-life story of speeding trains and snowy hills and a family band and the sound of cathedral bells singing carols across the River Wye at Christmastime. ○

BLUEBERRIES: BUSH TO BOWL

Their inner texture resonates with a certain tartness, while their deep hue conjures the warmth of a summer's day. This photographic journey begins with the origins of the berry, shedding light on the process from cultivation and harvesting to kitchen and bowl.

PHOTO ESSAY BY PARKER FITZGERALD & WORDS BY DANICA VAN DE VELDE

STYLING BY NATHAN WILLIAMS

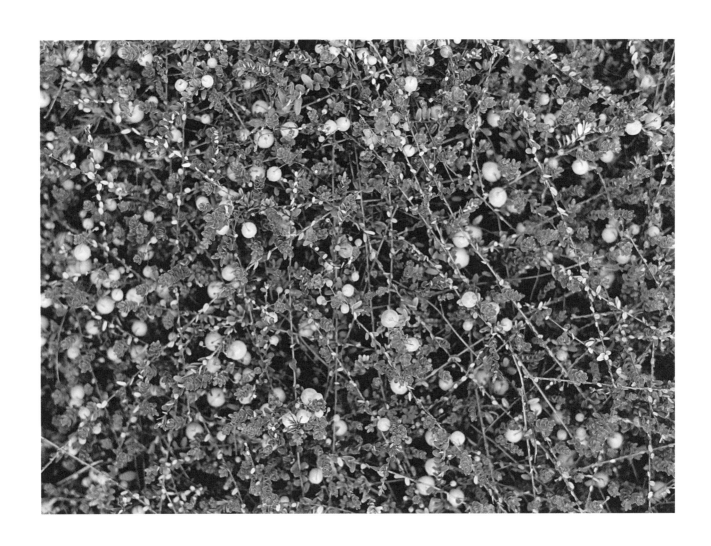

SPICED FIGS CRANBERRY SAUCE

INGREDIENTS

¾ cup sugar

½ teaspoon allspice

1 cup water

3 cups fresh (or frozen) cranberries

1 cup dried figs, roughly chopped

1 orange, zested and juiced

METHOD

Yields 4 cups.

In a large saucepan, combine sugar, allspice, and water over medium heat. Stir and simmer until the sugar is dissolved. To the pot, add the cranberries and figs. Increase the heat and bring to a boil. Cook uncovered for 5 minutes, until the cranberries begin to pop. Reduce heat and cook for 20 minutes longer, until thickened. Stir in the orange zest and juice. Set aside until ready to use.

Recipe by The Jewels of New York

View cranberry harvest at www.kinfolkmag.com/films

PIERRE JANCOU, CHEF AT VIVANT PARIS

INTERVIEW AND TRANSLATION BY ANNE STARK DITMEYER

PHOTOGRAPH BY PETRINA TINSLAY & STYLING BY ELODIE RAMBAUD

Under the wings of a former *oisellerie* [aviary, or bird shop] whose beautiful tiled interior serves as a reminder of its past, chef Pierre Jancou brings a fresh life to the 10th *arrondissement* of Paris with his resto/wine bar, Vivant. In his simple cuisine, the secret to his success comes from the ingredients he uses. And with a passion for *vin vivant*, a wine made in the most natural way possible from organically grown grapes, his knowledge serves him well.

Where are you from? Je suis très mélangé. I was born in Zurich. According to my passport I am Franco-Swiss. I speak French, Italian, Swiss-German, German, and English. My grandmother by my birth parents was French. When I was very young, I was adopted by an Italian family, so I am Italian by culture.

Why Paris? When I was eighteen, I came to Paris. It was my dream. My real grandmother was from Paris. I arrived in 1988. I worked for an awful *pizzeria* and then a *brasserie*, but I did work at Les Bains Douches at the end of their good years. In 1991, when I turned twenty-one, I received my inheritance and immediately invested it in La Bocca, an Italian *trattoria*. I did that for eight years with Aldo, who still works in the kitchen [of Vivant] today. My next project is a wine bar in the [same] neighborhood.

What is your connection to Italy? In 1999, I sold La Bocca and moved to Italy to learn my trade from Massimo Bottura, and take cooking courses. I also received a degree in natural cooking and learned how to keep the authenticity of the food. For instance, in Italy you never mix pasta with meat.

But I missed Paris. I love old Paris and the old areas of the city. My next project was La Crèmerie near Odeon, where we renovated everything. At La Crèmerie we imported all the products I had discovered in Italy—the *beau produits* that weren't available in Paris. I did that for five years, but then I started to miss cooking. In 2007 I started Racine. Everyone said the restaurant wouldn't work and it was a bad idea. It was in the Passage des Panoramas, and people would say the passageway was disgusting [at the time]. But Racine was a success, and still is.

At Vivant I have my special Berkel [machine] for slicing meats and a rare espresso machine for making it the Italian way.

What is your relationship with food? With my birth parents, it was as if I was born in a restaurant. I spent a lot of time there and it always has played an important role in my life. At one stage in my life I considered being a comedian, but I realized I am not capable of doing anything other than this. But perhaps one day I'll have my own vineyard.

What is your connection with wine? I became a *caviste* after I discovered natural wines, which are not something popular amongst our generation. Of particular interest were the *vins vivants* [alive or natural wines]. They change and evolve and must be kept at certain temperatures. You never have the same wine each year and a good grape dictates the wine. It is necessary to have a true *cave* [cellar] to respect the wine—part of the culture in France. These wines helped inspire the name of the restaurant, Vivant, as well the book—*Vin Vivant*—we published last summer. There is lots of great information on morethanorganic. com about these wines.

How do you choose your products? I work with several *founisseur* [suppliers] whose speciality and passion it is. For instance, Gianni Frasi has an admiration for pepper. That pepper is like a perfume and is very important in my cooking. The salt we use is a true *fleur du sel* from France. Aromatic herbs are also extremely important in what I cook. ○

HOW TO BE NEIGHBORLY: GIFT GIVING

WORDS BY JULIE POINTER

PHOTOGRAPHS BY LAURA DART & CARISSA GALLO

Open your eyes and your hands. Learning to be a generous neighbor is a practice of tangibility, and simply changing your physical posture is a good place to begin. Paying attention with your whole self turns your face outwards and upwards (and away from yourself), and keeps your hands at the ready to freely give, and freely receive.

If you're anything like me, you've experienced a season (or many) where everything feels hard, where living in a new city (or an old one) is lonesome, and empty, and you wonder if you'll ever put down roots and feel at home. Being at home is not merely geographic—it's having a sense of belonging, and feeling known, knowing others. When I feel out of place, it's easy for me to clam up, to close in on myself, and to begin ticking off the things I lack. At times, this inventory includes the carefree charisma to charm, the tight-knit community I crave, the invitations to cozy soup suppers and evenings spent around the fire. In short, I keep my head down, with my hands firmly clenched around my laundry list of wants.

During one particular season, in which I experienced this wanting most deeply, the thing that eventually changed me was not suddenly coming into a cache of friends, or resigning myself to self-pity; instead, my self-focused gaze shifted, and I began looking at and wondering about others around me. I quickly found that the antidote to discontent is examining what I *do* have, and sorting out how I might freely share it with others. While I know being neighborly extends beyond considering your

---

GIFT INSPIRATION

Cider Seasoning	*Music Mix for Chilly Evenings*	*Tin of Tea*
Bouquet of Leaves	*A Well-Loved Book*	*A Basket of Squash*
Pot of Soup	*A Cherished Recipe*	*Stack of Found Photos*
Dried Herbs	*Homemade Granola*	*Thrifted Woolen Blanket*
Bundle of Firewood	*A Hearty Plant*	*Collection of Candles*

---

street-mates, this seemed the most logical place for me to begin. Without going into the long details of fearful first meetings, cookies left at doorsteps (in the cover of night), and the constant trepidation of rejection, I found myself only a short time later being lavished with the generosity of those I had so nervously opened myself to. I shared Sunday morning French toast with the family next door, planted a garden with a new friend across the street, and started each day with greetings from the neighborhood children playing in the trees outside my window. Each of these new friendships was an unexpected gift, reminding me of the goodness of faithfully stepping toward these once-strangers in spite of my fear.

This act of unfolding oneself toward others is the beginning of the art of hospitality, an attitude that must be practiced daily to become habit-forming. The word "hospitality" has often been relegated to stiff, stuffy ideas of chocolates on pillows and pressing the sheets just so, but it has much more to do with the way you posture your body toward the world, and the people within it. One of my favorite ways of practicing hospitality—perhaps a favorite because it comes most naturally for me—is gift-giving. No fancy gifts, mind you; what I mean is more of a general open-handedness about the things I have, and the desire to share them with others. It's a strange paradox—the more I acknowledge my gratitude for the good things in my life, the more apt I am to want to give them away.

I love arriving at people's homes with a gift, whether for dinner, an overnight stay, or just a quick morning visit. Sometimes it's as simple as a jotted note of encouragement, a basket of strawberries, a few wildflowers plucked from the roadside on the way in. The point is not the extravagance of the gift, but rather, the intentionality of never arriving empty-handed. My home is speckled with these love-gifts from others—a mossy branch, a faded blue marble, a bit of driftwood, a matchbox, a postcard. I find joy in these simple objects because someone else has seen them with open eyes, and given them with open hands. The blessing of the offering can be such a surprise. ○

TWO

ENTERTAINING FOR TWO

○ ○

MAKING A TRIBE

As we sift through holiday memories of the past, it's easy to feel despondent over traditions lost and left in childhood. Rebecca encourages us to honor our families and these memories by maintaining traditions and starting our own.

WORDS BY REBECCA PARKER PAYNE

PHOTOGRAPHS BY PARKER FITZGERALD & STYLING BY MELISA MICHELE SIBLEY

Sometime in early December, somewhere within the hollers of the Blue Ridge Mountains, you could find us, wandering and weaving through long lines of pines and evergreens. Four siblings, our faithful dogs, and our daring captains: Mom and Dad. Our finest yearly tradition was born from the pinnacle of our mother and father's parenting career—their discovery of Christmas tree farms deep along the sloping ridges of the mountains. A mere two hours from our home, the hillside farms were light-years from the commercialism and consumerism that we lived among.

So every year we pilgrimaged to the Blue Ridge, to climb a mountainside and bring home the war-won tree. Our father, with verbal encouragement from his brood of children, pulled the tree down the hill, across a tiny creek, and perched it like an arbor trophy on the top of our faithful Suburban. It would be hailed *"A Christmas victory!"* by my father, despite the frozen, mittened hands, the carsick dogs, and the arduous process.

Traditions peppered our childhood lives, and the holidays meant they were only more salient. Something to remember our time by, something to look forward to, something to have that was special—something *ours*.

Our holiday season was characterized by these wild expressions of togetherness. In our tree travails, in our trips to Colonial Williamsburg to eat in the fire-lit taverns of yesteryear, in baking our apple-sausage quiches, in our matching Christmas bell necklaces. My siblings and I jingled as we danced through the holiday season.

We grew up unaware that our yearly routines were sowing and tending traditions. The rituals engulfed and enveloped us, and our youthful naiveté told us that this was just life—how our holidays were done. Only with age, and a healthy dose of selflessness, have we seen that this rhythm of delight and anticipation is the careful and thoughtful product of a family or parents that want to experience life together.

Because now, so much of our holidays are only remembering. I remember the food, I remember the traditions, and I remember the traditions revolving around food. I remember a few of the gifts, but with the most clarity I remember caroling on the back of a trolley, and tenderly pressing a cookie cutter into soft dough. I remember the brunches and the dinners, I remember the stillness, and I remember that feeling of warmth, closeness, unbounded joy. We number our memories, rewind and replay the moments that gave our holidays their meaning.

Now that I live independently, away from my childhood home, I find myself expecting the same rhythms, that the ones that comprised my youthful holidays, to be the footprint for this year's upcoming season. I remember it all, and still I want it to be the same. But things have changed. I haven't lived with my parents for years, which means they are no longer the leaders they once were of my holiday season. I do not have the abundant free time I did as a child, with which to make snowmen out of laundry detergent, or to hand-dip candles.

And this is where we are now, in this particular age. We are always busy, always moving from this

...we can take the traditions into our homes, draw them through the sieve of our personalities, sprinkle them with whimsy, mold them to our own relationships.

to that, here to there. We are young and filled. We understand why we had traditions, and should be thankful for them. We can even feel a draw to mourn the end of childhood traditions. All is right and expected of our growth and maturation, but we do not stay here. We are adults, and we are, in our best selves, independent, vibrant, thriving, and capable.

Holidays can take us in two directions. We can buy the presents, go to the parties, open the presents, clean the tissue paper from the floor. A dutiful ascension to an idea, a complacency to the expected. A casual nod to the time-honored celebrations, created outside of us. And we drift around each other in this harried time of giving and getting, making and doing.

Or, we can take the traditions into our homes, draw them through the sieve of our personalities, sprinkle them with whimsy, mold them to our own relationships. In doing so, we hold a respectful ownership of the season, where it cannot exist outside of us. Indeed, we are the daring captains of wonder and nearness in this time. And through our efforts, the holidays become intensely intimate, a seasonal experience tailored and defined by us who celebrate—our friends, our families, our own children.

This is how we measure the depth of our bated breath. This is how we calculate the expectancy of our hearts. The existence of our families and friendships are not entirely dependent on the existence of such activities and traditions, but the sustenance of such rituals is the soil in which we cultivate a deeper sense of commitment, history, and meaning. A group of casual friends becomes a community, a family becomes a tribe.

A few months ago, I started a new family altogether. A small family with tender roots. A family of just me and my man. A man with his own traditions, his own idiosyncratic holiday routines from growing up. He is the grown man that is memorialized in family photos up till about four years ago, sitting on his parents' stairs with his brothers, each sibling wearing matching pajamas. And although we don't have the same traditions, we both understand their role in making meaning of the holidays and our lives together. And we want to be a tribe.

In this place of adulthood, as a new family and as one-day future parents, we will cultivate a reason for hope and joy in all of our holiday seasons to come. I think it will involve long tables of food, homemade eggnog, and cranberry pies. It will involve storytelling and song singing. It will involve days of baking, and days of decorating. It will involve quietly lighting advent candles, and loudly spinning records. It will involve our community of friends and family, and it will be extravagant and hilarious and ours. It may even involve a borrowed tradition, a hauling of a tree down the side of a mountain. ○ ○

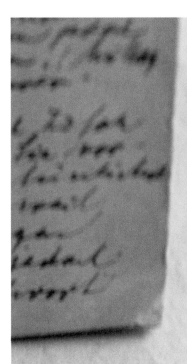

BUCHTELN: A FAMILY RECIPE

While so many things change from generation to generation, there are certain things that remain the same, like red cheeks when coming home after a winter walk in the snow, the tinge of excitement in the air as a grandfather tells adventure stories to his grandchildren, or the familiar feeling you have when looking at old photos of your family.

RECIPE AND PHOTOGRAPHS BY KATHRIN KOSCHITZKI

BLACKBERRY BUNS WITH WARM VANILLA SAUCE

(BROMBEERBUCHTELN MIT WARMER VANILLESAUCE)

A delicious recipe, given from generation to generation, may be baked in changing ovens, but its smell and taste will always remind us of the person that used to make it for us. We recognize that many of you will embrace the metric measurements of this recipe, but others of you will not. We have converted the recipe on our website, but wanted to honor Kathrin's family recipe in this volume.

Vanilla sauce
15 grams cornstarch
80 grams sugar
5 egg yolks
1 vanilla bean
500 grams milk
250 grams whipping cream

Dough
500 grams all-purpose flour

250 milliliters whole milk
50 grams sugar
42 grams fresh yeast
200 grams unsalted butter, softened
1 egg
generous pinch of salt

Filling
300 grams blackberries
.... and some powdered sugar to let it snow.

METHOD Pour the flour into a big bowl, and with your hands, form a small hollow in the middle. Warm the milk. Mix 5 tablespoons of the warm milk and 1 tablespoon of the sugar with the yeast and pour the mixture into the hollow. Allow to rise for about ten minutes.

Now add 120 grams of the butter, the remaining milk and sugar, and the egg and salt, and knead with your hands until you get homogenous dough. Form a ball, cover with a kitchen towel, and let rise in a warm place free from drafts, for 40 minutes.

In the meantime mix cornstarch, sugar, and egg yolks in a separate bowl. Halve the vanilla bean and scratch out the pith. In a big pot boil up milk, cream, vanilla pith, and scratched-out bean. Pour about 1/3 of the hot liquid into the egg-starch mixture; stir thoroughly, then pour this back into the original pot of milk-cream mixture and reheat over medium heat. Do not allow to boil. Stir thoroughly, until the sauce thickens. Remove from the stove. Let stand in the pot until ready to reheat for use, or store in the refrigerator if you will not use immediately.

When the dough has risen, knead again on the worktop. Form a roll and cut off about 20 equally big slices (each about 50 grams).

Press them flat individually with the palm of your hand and put 4–5 blackberries in the middle of each. Press the dough rims together to form a small ball. Put the buns into a buttered, oven-safe baking dish with the joined ends below (upside down). Cover with a kitchen towel and let rise for another 15 minutes.

Preheat a convection oven to 180°C. Melt the rest of the butter, gently brush it on the buns, and bake until golden-brown for 30–40 minutes. Let cool down and dust generously with powdered sugar. Serve with warm vanilla sauce. ○ ○

EVERYDAY SILVER

…while great-grandparents would surely be shocked by my modern-day sensibilities,
I would hope they'd appreciate the fact that these simple tools from their past
are a living part of my everyday.

How often do we rummage through our sideboards or kitchen drawers and wonder where we put those mischievous caviars forks? Or on a less formal day, those pesky cracker spoons—or asparagus tongs? And don't get me started on the pleasures of the perfect pickle fork, tomato server, or cream-soup spoon.

For many of us, it wasn't all that long ago that our relations—or in some cases, their help—kept meticulous track of countless place settings of silver. And, during down moments, had the pleasure of polishing and washing hundreds of different culinary implements. Oh, those were the good old days.

But in today's world, it's hard to know how the cocktail forks from yesteryear play into our everyday life. For some, they languish in safety deposit boxes—examined with casual interest by the inheriting generation, then in loving memory, driven across the state and deposited in a similar bank, in a similar vault, while they idly stand ready for another fifty years. Or there is the more permanent fate, one a tad more shocking to those who love familial treasures: silverware is sold to a refinery to capitalize on the panic-driven prices of precious metals. My family—the gatekeepers to hundreds of years of our collective culinary history—recently executed a series of Victorian place settings that didn't capture their aesthetic sensibilities. They weren't *Georg Jensen* after all. And who doesn't like a little extra walking-around money?

As for me, I've always enjoyed the pleasures of looking into my old mahogany sideboard and examining the contents. This piece of furniture has, thus far, survived five generations of boys—and their liberal use of BB guns. In fact, some

of its contents date back hundreds of years, worn thin by the pride of my people. But there remains the question of fish forks, cheese scoops, berry spoons. demitasse spoons, ruffled ladles, and the like. How do we make them work, or even identify their purpose, in today's informal, ready-made world, even when we've freed them from our eccentric great aunt, bachelor uncle, or banker's watchful eye?

Well, I'm not an expert. Let's be clear about that. But I am someone who likes to entertain. I also enjoy the layers of history—something that comes naturally to those of us that've inherited a mixed-and-matched, albeit .925-pure, world. Of course a little junior sleuthing on the Internet can prove helpful. Or you can always ask a more informed relation. Or, lastly, you can run the savage gauntlet and use your silverware however you prefer: categories be damned! I tend toward the latter—especially when searching for diminutive items to use during a cocktail party. There is no shortage of baby forks and spoons that circulate my living room. And other, larger items often make their way onto serving platters—be they proper meat forks or not.

In the end, I'm not sure the "how" is as important as the "why." And while great-grandparents would surely be shocked by my modern-day sensibilities, I would hope they'd appreciate the fact that these simple tools from their past are a living part of my everyday. Unlike most of my contemporaries, I have no use for common flatware. My family silver is my day-to-day fork, knife, and spoon—be they *demitasse*, game, or cocktail. And while the metal is slightly more tarnished than in might have been 200 years ago, it is no less cherished. And the meals, no less enjoyed.

WORDS BY NICHOLAS PARKER & PHOTOGRAPHS BY LAURA DART
PHOTOS TAKEN AT LOWELL SHOP IN PORTLAND, OREGON
PHOTOGRAPHED ARE OWNERS MAYA AND DINO

MORSELS WE KEEP AFTER THE MEAL

*How a shared moment of telling and listening can tie a stronger
bond between us—regardless of age.*

As a child, I spent a lot of time with older relatives. There was a whole band of greats and grands and thrice-removeds to visit. Often, we took weekend trips to my Aunt Ruth's house. My parents would pile my three sisters and me into our blue Dodge Caravan and make the trip to Long Island, crossing bridges and tunnels to get there; we passed the time with our noses pressed against the windows or into books until we found ourselves at her house in Port Washington.

A physician for sixty years, Aunt Ruth survived miraculously on a diet of ginger ale and English muffins, but when company came, she put out a spread. Cold cuts arranged on platters, slices of Portuguese bread in a silver bread basket, iceberg lettuce and beefsteak tomatoes, and crystal bowls of Miracle Whip, mustard, and sweet gherkins. The food wasn't fancy, but the presentation was.

As we ate, I mostly listened. It wasn't that I grew up in a family where children should be seen and not heard, but during those late-afternoon lunches there was just so much to hear. Aunt Ruth told stories of medical school in Texas in the 1920s, cross-country trips by train, and doll collections. Other times we would visit our cousins Grace and Bill at their home in Queens. Grace served *petit fours* on plates painted with forget-me-nots and told stories of sea captains and elevators in the Woolworth building. Still other times we would spend a morning at my grandparents' house where we listened to stories of a little boy scratching his name in the crown of the Statue of Liberty and playing stickball in alleys.

These trips to visit older relatives are no longer compulsory elements of my weekend, and as I have gotten older, the storytellers have left us for another realm. But I still seek moments of listening. Indeed, so impressed have I been by the tales of older folks, I focused much of my own graduate work on collecting stories for historical purposes. Last winter, in Providence, Rhode Island, I sat at the oilcloth-covered kitchen table of Stella Santos and recorded stories of factory work and Catholic nuns and cold-water flats. I was recording for an archive, but sitting at Stella's table, just listening, was what really mattered. The time we spent together did both of us good, more than either of us expected. She served lemon Bundt cake, baked that morning, and poured strong coffee. We slid my recording equipment to the side while we ate. She was seventy years my senior, but Stella's eyes lit up just as mine did with each retrieved memory.

These days, our cousin Mildred meets my sister, Cait, and me at the waffle place on the corner of 21st and 1st, when we all have the time. No matter how hard we try, she is always there first, waiting. She eats yogurt with fruit and as she talks, her wedding ring swirls around the thinness of her finger. Mildred tells us stories of Astoria and Bay Ridge, of learning how to drive, and of finding the time to read.

At each meal, Aunt Ruth began with the same secular grace: "Grab it and growl." At her table, and at all of these shared tables, the reason for gathering was to fill our bellies—but the secret source of nourishment was the stories themselves. The stories I love to hear, shared over meals and cups of tea, are not always stories of great accomplishment. They're not guaranteed to unlock deep mysteries or explain cultural norms, but there is comfort to be found in the way that the stories of one person's life can resonate across space and time. It's not the particulars that matter so much as their sharing: the mutual agreement that individual stories are worth the telling and worth the listening.

WORDS BY ERIN BOYLE & PHOTOGRAPH BY LISA WARNINGER
STYLING BY CHELSEA FUSS

TO BUILD A FIRE

The study of a skill requisite of winter warmth, entertaining, and true manhood.

WORDS BY DAVID WINWARD

PHOTOGRAPHS BY LEO PATRONE & STYLING BY NATHAN WILLIAMS

When you are driving through the mountains and you see a tepee, it is impossible not to say, "Look! A tepee!" There is something ingrained in our psyche that makes us love them. It is no wonder, then, that the tepee method is by far the most efficient fire-building method.

To make this type of fire, arrange kindling in a mound underneath larger logs to form a tepee over said kindling. Once the desired tepee configuration has been attained, light the kindling. If you are lazy, use a match and crumpled pages from a copy of your latest artisan quarterly magazine. If you are a purist, use flint and steel. If you are even purer than a purist, use the bow drill method. The fire will burn hottest at the top point of the tepee.

As the fire burns, the logs will fall in upon the fire. Since this formation creates the most heat, it is best to use if your wood is green or wet-ish. The only drawback is that your fire will consume a lot of wood. However, if you are a firebug or a pyromaniac (see: Impulse Control Disorders in the DSM-IV), this is not a drawback but a wonderful blessing.

If you are a fan of the western novels of Louis L'Amour, Zane Grey (see: *Riders of the Purple Sage*), or Cormac McCarthy (see: *Blood Meridian* or *All the Pretty Horses*), then the log cabin is the best method for you.

Stack layers of wood in alternating directions to form a cabin, using the wood like the Lincoln Logs you played with as a child. (Interesting side note: The inventor of Lincoln Logs was none other than Frank Lloyd Wright's son, John. Not Abraham Lincoln, as everyone supposes—but I hope that doesn't make you think less of Lincoln. He still accomplished quite a lot.) Even though this is called the log-cabin method, you still need to make a tepee inside of it to get it going. This, of course, is symbolic of the eternal cowboys-and-Indians struggle.

The log cabin creates a chimney effect, sucking in air from the bottom and releasing it through the top. If your fire doesn't seem to be getting enough oxygen, dig small holes under the walls or blow on the fire—but be careful not to singe your beard. The log-cabin method creates an ideal cooking environment of uniform heat. You can cook your tinfoil dinners, made from ingredients purchased from your local farmers' market, with confidence, knowing that the labors of the farmers and artisans won't be burned to a crisp.

The star method is particularly helpful when you are trying to conserve fuel, especially if you are sick and tired of tromping through the forest night after night in search of firewood. You curse yourself as you search because you had to pack an air mattress in the back of your car instead of firewood. Now your entire camping trip has turned into searching for firewood—wood that doesn't need chopping, because you left your brand-new axe sitting at home.

To build this type of fire, first arrange logs in a star shape around a center point, which is where you will place the kindling. Once the fire has started, you can move logs in and out of the fire to increase or decrease the heat as you see fit, which conserves your wood.

Its very name makes you think that it is a temporary method, or one that you would need to use only in adverse weather conditions. When I got my Wilderness Survival merit badge in Scouting, I had to build a lean-to and sleep in it. That night it rained, and my lean-to didn't keep the rain out; I didn't sleep; I was eaten alive by mosquitos; and some Tenderfoot scared a skunk just outside the camp, and the smell lingered all night long. The lean-to method is a lot like that night—don't use it unless, of course, you really, really need to.

To build a lean-to fire, push a green stick into the ground at a 30-degree angle. It should be pointing in the direction of the wind. Put tinder underneath. "Lean" sticks along the main stick. Light, and add more kindling as needed. If it doesn't work, I'm not surprised, because it's a terrible method. And if you are in a life-or-death situation, I don't have much sympathy because you probably did something foolish to get yourself where you are. And please don't tell me your sob story because I read Jack London's *To Build a Fire* and I shed enough tears over that man and his dog. I'm sure he was using the lean-to method.

If you are like me, you have never used this method. If you *have* used this method, you are a fire-building superstar. You are like the Survivorman of your neighborhood. You don't even need to read any further.

For the rest of us, to build a cross-ditch fire, you need a shovel or similar caveman contrivance. Dig a three-inch-deep cross in the ground. Place your kindling in the center and build a pyramid over the top of it. The ditch will let air in to feed the fire.

I'm not sure what scenario calls for this type of fire. But if you are the type of person that knows everything and brings a fold-up, ten-pound shovel with you on a backpacking trip, then this fire is for you. You can lecture everyone on the benefits of proper airflow for fires. When you have exhausted the "airflow vectors" dissertation, you can tell everyone how many miles your pedometer said you hiked that day, or lecture them on the benefits of moisture-wicking socks.

If you like contemplating how the ancient Egyptians built the pyramids, or if you are a fan of the Tom Robbins book *Still Life With Woodpecker*, the pyramid method is for you. (If you are a redhead and haven't read this book yet, you should.)

Construction of the pyramid is similar to that of the log cabin. The layers just get smaller as you go toward the top—like a pyramid! Alas, you will not use a tepee in this method, although some tepee-method fanatics may argue that a pyramid is technically the shape of a tepee. Your smallest sticks and kindling will be at the pyramid's point. This is where you will light the fire, and it will burn down through all the layers upon itself.

---

7. INEPT METHOD If you are extremely lazy and/or incapable of building a fire, you may just want to bring one of those easy-start logs. Lighter fluid also works wonders, as does gasoline. Hairspray and a lighter is also a fun diversion, but probably not very safe, effective, or good for the ozone. ○○

Toes and nose and cheeks would be only touched by the frost, for the fire was beginning to burn with strength. He was feeding it with twigs the size of his finger. In another minute he would be able to feed it with branches the size of his wrist, and then he could remove his wet foot-gear, and, while it dried, he could keep his naked feet warm by the fire, rubbing them at first, of course, with snow. The fire was a success. He was safe.[1]

—JACK LONDON, TO BUILD A FIRE

THE BAKER BROTHERS

INTERVIEW AND PHOTOGRAPHS BY ROSA PARK

Tom and Henry Herbert are fifth-generation bakers and brothers from the beloved Cotswold-based Hobbs House Bakery and Butchery (Tom runs the bakery, and Henry the butchery next door). They star in the popular Channel 4 TV series, *The Fabulous Baker Brothers*, and released a cookbook by the same name earlier this year, to much fanfare.

The embodiment of great modern British cuisine, Tom and Henry celebrate and preserve their proud English heritage with the food they prepare, and believe that all gatherings should feature homemade bread at the centre of the table. Conversation should flow around the bread, as people tear big hunks off the loaf. It doesn't matter whether the bread gets recognition or not; the point is that it's there, and it's filling the home with the scent of warm, fresh baking.

The brothers revive and reinvent classic British dishes. They understand simple pleasures—like fish finger sandwiches, bread sauce with roast chicken, and beef stew—and know how to give them tweaks that make each meal more enticing, like serving sourdough pancakes with poached fruit and *crème fraiche.*

Their collective cooking reads like a recipe for a delicious life, and their passion for food is infectious. From them I've learned that a BLT done right is a thing to behold and devour, and a great beef Wellington can be mind blowing—especially with *foie gras.* Representing five generations' worth of Herbert's bread knowledge, Tom and Henry demonstrate how mixing flour and water can lead to a lifetime of peace and loaf.

TOM HERBERT

What is British baking to you? For me, British baking is all about real bread. I'm an ambassador for the Real Bread Campaign. In a nutshell, it's bread that's made with simple, natural ingredients—bread that's easier to digest and something that's been touched by a craftsperson. At Hobbs House, we use four words to describe the bread we make: flour, water, time, and passion. I really believe you need all four to make bread that's worth traveling for.

What is the difference between British and French baking? British baking is much more inclusive and has an honesty to it that strikes a chord with people, just the way that sitting around a campfire does. I believe that wherever there is good British food, there should be real bread. But that doesn't require a plaited *brioche*; it can be something simple that's made with time, passion, and love. If you gather loved ones around a table, it should be around a loaf that you've made yourself or from a bakery that's made it with integrity.

What role does bread play in gatherings? Bread brings everything and everyone together. The word "companion" is made up of three Latin roots: "*com*," which is friends, "*panis*," which is bread, and "*ion*," which is doing. So companionship is all about friends, bread, and being together. That's where bread is at its best—when it's loved and shared.

What is your favorite Hobbs House bread? It would have to be our Sherston overnight dough bread. It's made to my great-grandfather's recipe. We still make it the same way. The story goes that he used to sleep on the dough bin and it'd tip him off in the morning when it was time to start baking.

If you were a bread, which one would you be? I'd be the tiger bread, because it's misunderstood and has an interesting story to it. The tiger bread goes back 400 years in Cornwall, before people knew what tigers looked like. Back then, they were hearing stories of these exotic tigers, so they created a bread that they thought resembled the pattern of a tiger. Of course it looks more like a leopard or a giraffe.

What is the perfect small gathering for you? It's about being with the people you love. And the location is key—somewhere that feels like home and has soul. There needs to be good food and wine, exciting cocktails with fantastic music, and the promise of dancing afterwards.

What is your favorite food memory? For my mum's 50th birthday, we invited 50 people and threw her a surprise party at the barn on the farm where my mum and dad live. We made the setting similar to the film *Where the Wild Things Are*, when his bedroom turns into the woods. We made a massive seafood bisque and fed our guests with hot bread and soup.

Your finest moment to date? On my birthday this year, my son Milo baked me a loaf of bread from scratch. He got up at 6:14 am and used my white bread recipe card. He put it in the oven before he went to school. I was so touched.

———————————————— HENRY HERBERT ————————————————

What is British baking to you? Something like a cottage loaf. It's a bit fuddy-duddy, and is a big, crusty white loaf. When they're made well, they're wicked. And Britain is full of cottages—well, at least, it's what everyone thinks it's full of.

What is the difference between British and French baking? French *patisserie* is more refined in terms of technique. English baking, on the other hand, is more hefty and stodgy. We're more famous for our sliced white rather than delicate pastries. We're also like magpies—we love influence from other cultures, so we've collected things and made them our own. A British bakery is much more diverse. We offer everything from a cottage loaf and a *baguette* to a rye loaf, pita, and *naan* bread.

What is your favorite Hobbs House bread? For sandwiches, I'd go for our Sherston. I also love our seeded spelt loaf—it's squishy and moist and a great accompaniment to cheese.

If you were a bread, which one would you be? I would probably be the Behemoth. It's larger than life, it's exuberant, and slightly ridiculous—cutting it is a nightmare. But it's good fun and it's got presence; I don't know if I've got that though…

What is the perfect small gathering for you? It would be me cooking for a selection of people—some friends and family. I love cooking for others. I'd serve rustic, family-style dishes, featuring meats and whole fishes. I'd finish with a nice pudding and make sure there's enough drinks, coffee, and of course, great cheese.

Give us a cool butchery fact. We sell 2,000 handmade sausages a week, which is impressive for a small shop like ours.

What is your favorite food memory? Eating hot peaches on the beach in Greece, and tasting the sweetness of the peach mixing in with the saltiness of the beach.

What would you be doing right now if you weren't answering these questions? I'd be drinking cocktails at home, probably cooking some fish on the barbecue—just enjoying this beautiful Sunday.

Your finest moment to date? Getting married. ○○

FEW

ENTERTAINING FOR A FEW

∘ ∘ ∘

OUR TREE: THE GRACEFUL EVERGREEN

*With the inbreath of wintertime, we gather with unhurried intent for quiet observance,
merrymaking, and a celebration of the evergreen gifts of rest and renewal.*

WORDS BY LOUISA THOMSEN BRITS

PHOTOGRAPHS BY LEO PATRONE & PARKER FITZGERALD

To bring evergreen trees, boughs, and sprigs into our homes is more than tradition.
It is an act of hope and recognition, passed from generation to generation, culture to
culture—a simple ritual that invites magic and healing, that breathes life, that lifts
the spirit and makes things happen.

Our small tree stands at the heart of our celebration, holding out branches lit with candles in a silent gesture of warmth and generosity. It is a point of contemplation and a symbol of quiet hope. Its spiral of evergreen branches and whorls of fine needles remind us that life flows and is constant. We have decorated it with red wooden hearts, wax stars, pale straw snowflakes, and white lights. In return, it offers us ancient wisdom from the past, to make sense of our present and guide us in the future.

There is promise in the gifts we have tucked beneath the tree and in the way we yield to the moment and to each other. We allow ourselves to be childlike and to be touched by the reassuring presence of our tree, by its elemental nature and upright beauty. The air is full of the clean earth and spice scent of resin. We are lifted out of time, beyond everyday life, to a place of stillness and wonder.

Beginning with the youngest child, each one of us chooses a carol or song. We begin to dance. Faster and faster. Shadows race across the walls. We remember the spirit of the darksome earth, the fertile soil where our tree took root, and acknowledge the shadow that exists in each of us. Together we face the darkness outside and within. Our small circle of light shines out into the night.

Inside our home and outside in gardens, parks, and forests, evergreen trees stand sentinel as the year moves quietly forward toward spring. Signs of early growth in the luminous green tips of pine branches remind us of the possibility of regeneration and birth.

To bring evergreen trees, boughs, and sprigs into our homes is more than tradition. It is an act of hope and recognition, passed from generation to generation, culture to culture—a simple ritual that invites magic and healing, that breathes life, that lifts the spirit and makes things happen. According to folklore, pine is the giver of foresight, setting us on the right course for the coming year. When we gather yew and holly to hang above our doorways, we echo the steps our ancestors took to ward off evil and to heal the sickness we feel when we are trapped inside by the weather. The smoke and sap of evergreen trees clear our dark moods, self-blame, aches, guilt, and tension, and create space for positive thought and action.

Our tree, and the precious transient gift of its presence, changes our home. It feels like a blessing. We treat it as a companionable houseguest, waking each day to enjoy its quietude with our morning coffee. Some nights, we carry quilts and pillows into the drawing room to sleep close to it and to treasure its company until Epiphany. Then we light the candles one more time, remove and wrap each decoration for safekeeping, sweep up fallen needles, and carry the tree outside. Each branch is kept for kindling. We collect the sweet scented logs cut from its straight trunk, cast-off and worn-out clothes, and thick branches of slow-burning yew to build a Yule fire that frees the spirit of the solar year. When the fire has burned out, the ash is worked into the soil to prepare for planting and new growth.

We trust that the tree was glad to hold our garlands and candles, to share its own harmonious beauty, and bring us its message, "What I do is be me. That's why I am here." We remain touched by its grace. It has helped us look inward, and has showed us how to flow outward. The gratitude we feel for the gift of its life, and our own, will permeate our year.

When we walk the soft paths of an evergreen forest, look up through the branches of a towering pine, or place a small sprig of holly on the mantelpiece, we know the comfort of renewal and continuity; we take time to contemplate our contribution to life, to celebrate our connection to each other, and to feel the silky bonds between us and the natural world that offers us shelter, warmth, protection, wisdom, and hope. ○○○

Our tree, and the precious transient gift of its presence, changes our home. It feels like a blessing.
We treat it as a companionable houseguest, waking each day to enjoy its quietude with our morning coffee.

When we walk the soft paths of an evergreen forest, look up through the branches of a towering pine...

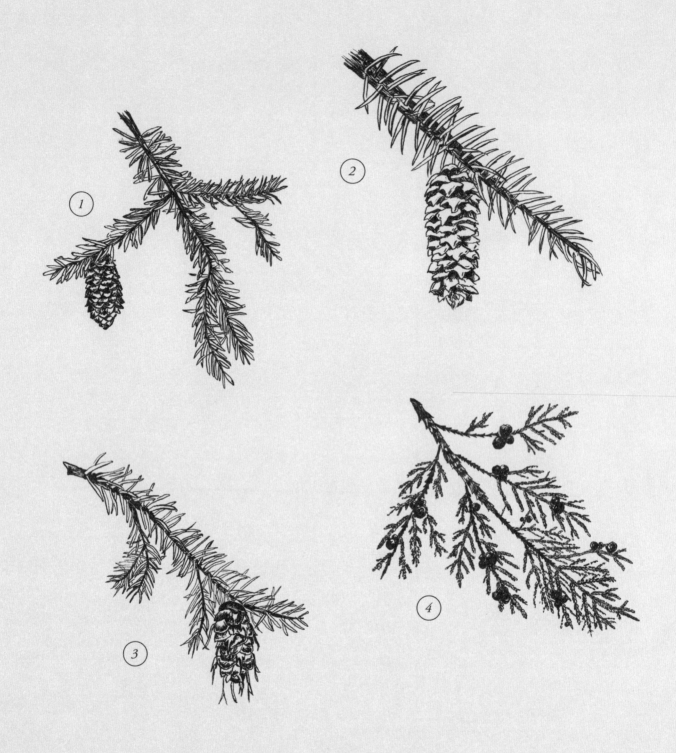

EVERGREEN FORAGING GUIDE
ILLUSTRATIONS BY JOY KIM

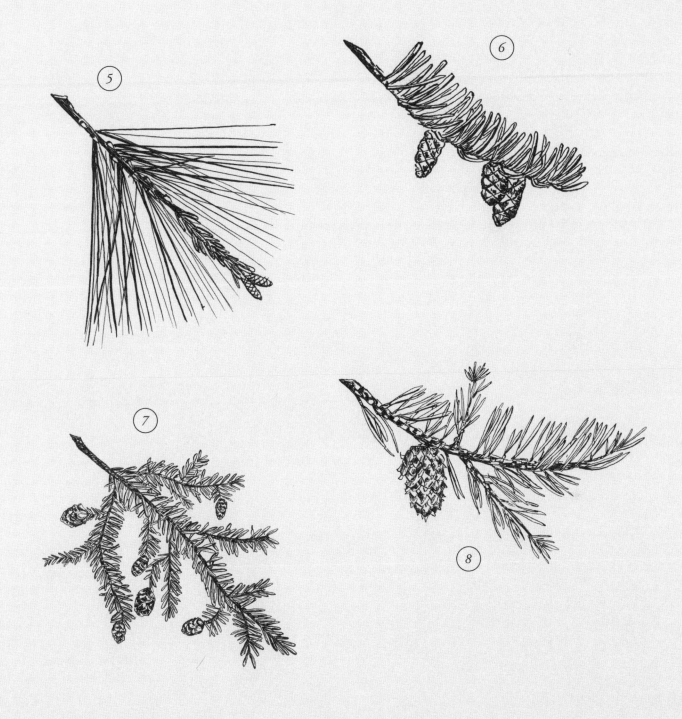

1. Balsam Fir   4. Eastern Red Cedar   7. Hemlock
2. Colorado Blue Spruce 5. Eastern White Pine   8. Virginia Pine
3. Douglas Fir   6. Fraser Fir

HOME USES FOR THE EVERGREEN TREE

COMPILED BY MEGAN MARTIN

GIFT GIVING

1. Decorate packages with evergreen cuttings.

2. Collect needles in a small sachet for drawers or linen cabinets.

3. Make a pine-scented infused oil for someone that is not able have a tree in their home during the holidays.

4. Stamp holiday cards using a small evergreen sprig and paint.

DECORATING

1. Construct a wreath with branches and twine to hang on a door.

2. Display attractive branches over doorways.

3. Tuck small cuttings around picture frames.

4. Make small branch impressions in salt dough, and bake for a non-edible holiday decoration.

5. Display candles on the trimmings from the bottom of the tree trunk.

EDIBLES

It is best to use foraged or non-sprayed trees for edible uses—make sure no chemicals have been near the tree. Also note that not all evergreens will be edible. Please confirm that the plant you intend to eat is not poisonous before consuming. Pregnant women should not consume the evergreen edibles, and all others should consume them in moderation.

1. Pour boiling water over needles for an aromatic tea.

2. Strip the lower half of a spruce sprig and use the stem as a skewer for cheese or olives.

3. Garnish a large serving platter with small branches.

4. Fill a mason jar with needles, citrus peels, and honey. Strain after infusing for a few weeks. Serve syrup on ice cream or other desserts.

5. Place two evergreen sprigs in a mason jar filled with vinegar. Store for a few weeks, in a cool, dark place, then strain and use in cooking or salad dressings.

6. Replace rosemary with evergreen sprig tips in a holiday poultry meal.

7. Infuse a bottle of gin with a few tree cuttings—let rest for twenty-four hours and then remove to serve.

EVERGREENS TREES TO USE

1. *Douglas Fir:* Great for sachets, simmering for scent, infused oils, and household decorating. When used for tea, use needles only (can be dried needles).

2. *Balsam Pine or White Pine:* Best for teas (can crush or chop needles first), gin infusion, honey infusion, print making, and salt dough impressions.

3. *Spruce or Blue Spruce:* Best for food garnish, in place of rosemary and thyme, gin infusion, vinegar infusion, and household decorating.

PLEASING THE SENSES

1. Simmer evergreen sprigs and cinnamon sticks in water on the stovetop for wintery smells.

2. Make a relaxing bath tea by placing pine needles in a tea ball into your bath.

SIMMER POTS

WORDS BY KATIE SEARLE-WILLIAMS & PHOTOGRAPH BY LEO PATRONE

When I was growing up, my mom would put a pot of water on the stove and simmer cinnamon sticks and orange peels to make our home a transcendent wonderland. This is such a simple way to create a cozying effect.

WONDERFUL COMBINATIONS

2 tablespoons whole cloves
2 cinnamon sticks
5 star anise
1 orange peel

—

3 sprigs evergreen or handful pine needles
2 cinnamon sticks
2 tablespoons whole cloves
2 bay leaves
2 pieces orange peel
2 pieces lemon peel

—

2 tablespoons whole cloves
1 teaspoon nutmeg

—

5 bay leaves
1 tablespoon whole cloves
2 cinnamon sticks

—

⅛ cup whole cloves
⅛ cup allspice

2 cinnamon sticks
1 teaspoon vanilla

—

1 cup lavender
1 teaspoon anise
1 tablespoon nutmeg
1 tablespoon whole cloves
1 cinnamon stick

—

a few drops of vanilla
orange peels

START YOUR OWN SIMMER POT TRADITION Fill a pot half full with water, bring to a boil, add your favorite ingredients, turn heat down, and simmer all day, adding water when needed. There are no strict parameters—feel free to mix ingredients and vary the amounts to your liking.

A FEW TIPS
1. Refrigerate your simmer mixture and reuse it for up to one week. Add water as needed.
2. Keep your orange, lemon, and lime peels, as well as apple skins (dry them out first before storing in a container). Use these ingredients with various spice combinations suggested above or create your own.
3. For fruit juices, herbs, and spices that are ending their life cycle, don't throw them out—just add them to your pot.
4. Set a reminder for every 30 minutes so you remember to top off your water. Do not leave your simmer pot going when you leave the house.

FOR STORAGE For a mix to keep on hand, try this easy-to-store recipe. Combine all ingredients (2 cups dried rosemary, 2 cups dried lavender, 1 cup dried eucalyptus leaves, ½ cup dried peppermint or spearmint, ½ cup dried bay leaves), keep stored in an airtight container, and add 1 cup mix per 3 cups boiling water. ○ ○ ○

STAFF LUNCHES WITH THE MAST BROTHERS

INTERVIEW BY JULIE POINTER & PHOTOGRAPHS BY GENTL & HYERS

Given the amount of time that we all spend at our workplaces, it seems natural that this space in our lives might also produce a deep sense of connectivity and community with those working around us. While we may not share commonalities with our workmates in all areas of life, we may, at the very least, feel a sense of shared purpose in working toward a unified goal, which can often supersede more trivial lifestyle differences.

One of the ways to build this familial, close-knit feeling is to set aside time in the workday to gather around a meal—and better yet, to prepare it together. There is hardly a more satisfying way to alleviate the stresses of the day than to focus on creating a dish to be communally enjoyed; your own worries may quiet merely by paying attention to the person chopping vegetables at your side. Having a midday meal together around a common table seems a simple thing, but it can be the key to cultivating a vibrant, healthy community of workers that are connected not only through a shared workplace, but also through shared experiences.

One such business that has encouraged eating together since its inception is Mast Brothers Chocolate, which is located in the Williamsburg neighborhood of Brooklyn, New York. The following brief conversation was with Derek Herbster, one of Rick and Michael Mast's loyal compatriots.

Is there a shared ethos among the Mast workers that unifies the team? The ethos, from the beginning, has always been to keep making the best chocolate that we possibly can, constantly tasting everything every step of the way together through the process. We have also grown to be a big family under one roof.

What's the general vibe like among the Mast crew in the day-to-day occurrences? The vibe day-to-day is to always get the job done, of course, but while that's happening, lots of jokes and laughs. Some good-natured ribbing, I guess is what some may call it.

How and when did the tradition of eating lunch together start at the office/factory? Do you all share the cooking? Really since the beginning days—Rick Mast (being a trained chef) always kind of led the charge in the kitchen, and would always prepare lunch for whomever was working with him and his brother that day. It really just grew and grew from there. We all cook, though some are better than others, of course, and tend to get voted to cook (just because we know it will be good). It's basically whomever feels like making something great that day; it always changes. Along with that, though, we also have an hour-long break after lunch to do what we please with, which is really something that I feel other businesses should get into.

What is the Mast Brothers factory's role in the context of the bigger neighborhood/community? Since we were the first bean-to-bar chocolate makers in Brooklyn, I'd say we have a pretty strong role in the community here in Williamsburg. It's a very tight-knit community/scene here in Brooklyn, which is great, because there's a lot of support for each other going on. Really something special.

How do you see the community-feel of your space affecting the larger purpose of what Mast is doing? When you walk into the Mast Brothers factory, we want you to feel that you are part of the process and what is being created right in front of you. Which is why we have always had our retail shop connected to our factory, so when you walk in you get a sense of what's going on. ○○○

WINTER WEEKENDS

*The arrival of winter is cause for celebration, cozy weekends,
and a warming chocolate beverage.*

WORDS BY YOLANDA DE MONTIJO & PHOTOGRAPHS BY LAURIE FRANKEL
STYLING BY LISA MOIR

For a Northern Californian, winter can exist all year round, depending on where you find yourself—there are chilly San Francisco summers, cool peninsula autumns, the still-brisk spring mornings in Sonoma and Napa, and everywhere, on almost any day, our Pacific fog rolling through.

When winter finally comes, the fog and mist stay longer, as though they are welcomed at last, and you embrace their presence. When winter comes, we pull out sweaters and blankets, shake them of their hibernation, and drape ourselves in layers and layers. When winter comes, we go through the bottom kitchen drawers and pull out the big pots for soups, sauces, stews, *tamales,* mulled wine, hot chocolate, *champurrado.* The inside of the house knows to make up for the weather outside, for the starkness of the trees, for the stillness of the air, for the sounds of dry leaves and branches snapping underfoot. The inside of the house grows warmer from all of us, louder, more colorful, more chaotic maybe, messier maybe. There are crusted rain boots by the door, bits of branches and wood chips from the wood stack by the fireplace, cups with coffee stains in odd places, mud tracks, jackets hanging over chairs, blankets crumpled on the sofa, toys and toy parts everywhere—like a perpetual winter weekend that we don't want to end.

When my parents come up for a weekend, I can only tell our son, who is almost three, they are coming a few hours before they arrive, or he will want them there immediately. My mom and I will spend most of our time in the kitchen, staying warm, cooking, cleaning, talking, not talking, laying out the food, then putting away the leftovers, contented with our duties. For dinner, we dress the table, light the candles, and pull out all our big vintage serving dishes and serving spoons. It takes a day to make dinner, and it's over in less than an hour, though we try to linger, to prolong it, until the food is cold and we pick at it directly from the serving dish.

I remember the growing excitement that winter brought, when my brother and I were small, as the holidays came closer each week. Every weekend was special because it was almost the holidays, and our parents indulged us more with food or behavior, as though they finally gave in to us being wild, staying up later, eating too many sweets. I love winter weekends for the warmth that builds in the house all day, for the sweet indulgences, for times that are a mix of family and friends, and I still feel a secret sense of excitement for the holidays to come, and for future holidays. ○○○

CHAMPURRADO

INGREDIENTS

¼ cup *masa harina*

2 cups water

2 cups milk

1 round Mexican chocolate,
coarsely chopped

2 cones *piloncillo*
(about one ounce each),
chopped (or substitute 2 ounces
granulated sugar)

1 pinch ground anise seed (optional)

METHOD

Serves 2-4.

In a large pot, over medium-high heat,
mix the *masa harina* together with
the water using a whisk,
until it is thoroughly blended.

Add the rest of the ingredients,
and whisk vigorously until chocolate
and sugar are melted and blended and
a slight froth forms.

Ladle into mugs.
Serve hot, sip slowly, and enjoy.

ABOUT *Champurrado* is a warm
Mexican drink made from *masa harina*
and chocolate. Though *masa harina* is
used to make *tamales*, this drink is nothing
like a blended *tamale* and more like a rich,
thickened hot chocolate.

SYNCHRONICITY

WORDS AND PHOTOGRAPHS BY OLIVIA RAE JAMES

I grew up in the kitchen. It is here that my mom and I would spend hours upon hours. It was our comfort zone, our sacred place. Anything could be said in the kitchen, and when there was nothing, there was cooking.

My mom can do no wrong in the kitchen. She balks at recipes and embraces spontaneity. She lets ingredients speak for themselves, even for the most modest of dishes: roasted beets, purple and golden; cauliflower soup with a hint of truffle; pasta filled with basil from her garden. She has fed my family with gusto for longer than I can remember; my sister with her peculiar cravings (peanut butter on eggs?) and my dad who genuinely believes every dish is the best he's ever had. Mindful of taste, health, color, and origin, no detail goes overlooked in my mom's kitchen.

We cook for the ritual of it—the methodical chopping of onions and consequent teary eyes; the weight of a sturdy knife striking the butcher block as we watch crumbs form under the baguette; the hushed sounds of Nina Simone mingled with the steady murmur of the oven fan. These elements together, simple as they are, render us weak at the knees. We feel a purpose and a peace here unlike we do anywhere else. In the kitchen, we are content.

Whether we are cooking elbow-to-elbow or are separated by oceans, my mom and I continue to assume this shared energy in the kitchen. And now when I cook in my own kitchen, every eccentricity I possess or method I prefer feels like a warm salute to her.

Time spent in the kitchen should be cherished—not only as a means to our lifeblood, but as a detail of our everyday that graces us with sustenance and beauty. And in the end, the actual food is only a small part of that.

TRUFFLE CAULIFLOWER SOUP

1 head cauliflower

1 tablespoon olive oil

4 cups vegetable broth

3 tablespoons heavy cream

1 tablespoon ground nutmeg

2 tablespoons truffle butter

(available in most specialty food stores)

coarse sea salt and ground black pepper to taste

METHOD Preheat your oven to 400°F. Roughly chop cauliflower and place on a sheet pan lined with parchment paper. Lightly coat cauliflower in olive oil and generously sprinkle with sea salt. Roast cauliflower until slightly browned, about 30 minutes.

Transfer cauliflower to a large pot on medium heat; add vegetable broth and cream. Using an immersion blender, blend mixture until smooth. Add nutmeg, truffle butter, and salt and pepper to taste, and serve. ○○○

EATING REVERENTLY

WORDS BY NIKAELA MARIE PETERS

*It is important to be awake to the sacred reasons people gather around food,
to sacred histories of food, if we want to best appreciate and care for our traditions
and best approach our gatherings with grace and reverence.*

B ecause food is tradition (flavours hold our memories and our pasts) and because food physically is the source of life, the ways of imbuing it with spiritual significance are as varied as human experience itself. It is important to acknowledge this in order to properly appreciate the bounty of our own tables, and the traditions of our own kitchens. Although many of the ways food and gathering retain spiritual significance are religious, some are not necessarily so: salt preserves; olive oil anoints; tea steeps; the crop in the field hopes. There is a Spanish proverb that reads, "Bread is relief for all kinds of grief." These most basic ingredients in our gardens and cupboards have the power to preserve and anoint and steep and relieve and hope. Intrinsic to food and eating, therefore, is thankfulness and magic, whatever the beliefs of the eater.

THE WORLD'S LARGEST RELIGION began with a meal. There was a large enough room for the people invited. There was a jug of water. There were bowls and loaves of bread and cups and vessels of wine. There were prayers and speeches; there was a song and an argument. The night before he was killed, Jesus ate supper with his friends. One might argue that there was born a sacrament so central to Christianity, that the Church itself was born that night. The Eucharist, many Christians believe, reenacts both that meal and the sacrifice Jesus made on humankind's behalf—offering forgiveness and collapsing the divide between God and humanity. For Christians, during communion, all distances are crossed, all boundaries blurred. Life unites with death; spirit with body; meaning with fact; the profane with the sacred; the host with the guest.[2] But also, as perhaps non-Christians more likely observe, the ritual is simply bread and wine. There might be a tablecloth or a candle, there might be a prayer, but the bread comes from the same place as does our morning toast, baked by the same young baker who works at the bakery down the street.

Ryan is that young baker. He talks about bread the way he talks about philosophy. His voice is nostalgic and curious. He talks with his hands. He jumps, in the same breath, from Thomas Aquinas to a recipe for bread to the Book of Exodus. It is sometimes hard to follow. And while he talks, he prepares to bake bread for his local parish's Eucharist the following day. He ties his apron on, he pulls out his rolling pin, and he covers his head with a hat. He lines up three forks next to a bread cutter. These actions are the opposite of his capacious sentences; they are deliberate, even meticulous. They are easy to follow.

"Every time I bake, I am searching for a certain sameness," he starts. "Sameness is interesting because it is about unity. About the many becoming one." He offers that baking bread is more of a guiding, or a training, than it is a making: "You can control all the outside variables of baking bread, but at the centre is something you cannot control. The yeast lives on its own. There is a mystery there." In other words, baking is part question, part answer. Like philosophy, baking is inquiry: something uncertain (questions, ingredients) becomes something definite (an answer, a cake). The answer is so whole and complete, the question is unthinkable. But we do not know all the pieces of the question or the answer. There is mystery in our asking, and even more mystery in our answers. We do not control everything in the baking process, just like we do not control everything in faith: we ask questions, but at a certain, we have point have to give up reason—control—to get faith.[3] And, according to Ryan, baking, like any search for truth, requires faith.

When I ask Ryan how baking bread for the church is different from baking multigrain for sandwiches, he responds simply. "In many ways, there is no difference. The bread becomes a part of you either way." In other words, we are what we eat. This is physically true. It may or may not, depending on what you believe, be spiritually true.

Only food—all necessary, visible, divisible, an external object which becomes internal, and which then turns into the very substance of the eater—could give rise to such a clear yet mysterious and effective ritual. MARGARET VISSER, THE RITUALS OF FOOD[4]

THE APPROACH WE TAKE to feeding one another in our individual homes, the manner in which we gather around the table, the unspoken dividing and sharing of responsibilities, the inarticulate daily habits, are all bound by ritual and rich with ceremony. Like religious practices, these details reveal hidden graces and express our repeating and consistent gratitude. They can reflect the general peace of a household, or be the cause of divide and discord. These "ways of doing things" are not without controversy because they are specific and savoury. Just like religious sacraments, their power to include, to ground and form our identities, to draw an imaginary line around our households, is as profound as their power to exclude. In *our* house, we are unified by the way we give and receive acts of comfort, the timings of our comings and goings, the type of milk we buy, the type of cereal. At their most basic, these housekeeping details are a simple system of kindnesses holding together the fabric of our families.[5] At their most complicated, they are an intricate web of histories and beliefs, as paradoxical and tangled and esoteric as any religion. To grow bored of our tables and foods, therefore, would not only be sad and unhealthy, it would be, in every sense of the word, irreverent. ○○○

HOLIDAY HEALTH RULES

*This time of year can be busy; remember to take yourself
less seriously, and your food more so.*

1. Given the chance—say, at a holiday gathering—to play with younger cousins, children of your own, or other young ones, do it wholeheartedly. Chase, get stuck on children's slides, lose at a game of tag—whatever it takes.

2. Anything that comes in a can or a box better not be the main dish.

3. Microwaves are boring. Use them less.

4. Incorporate a new activity into your holiday travel: swim in a crystal-blue lake, fly down a snowy mountain peak with nothing but a pair of undersized skis and a wild-eyed, I'm-here-to-raise-hell expression on your face.

5. Always keep learning, reading, striving to know the world: an active mind will require an active body to keep up with it.

6. Take up a winter sport from your childhood, on a Saturday with friends, and find out whether you fall on your ass or find yourself the complete king of the day.

7. Call, write, visit, and talk to those that you love or that inspire you; positive people will make you that much more excited to be around and healthy for 100 years.

8. Be around nature—after all, it's shrinking every day. Listen to birds, play with a family pet, go on a trek to wild parts (besides the in-laws').

9. Drive or walk to somewhere you love before the sun rises. Seeing a day unfold will stay with you, for a long time.

10. Always visit the produce aisle of the markets where you shop, and try a new fruit or vegetable each time.

11. Never underestimate the quality of simple foods.

WORDS BY TRAVIS ROGERS & PHOTOGRAPHS BY LEO PATRONE

STYLING BY NATHAN WILLIAMS

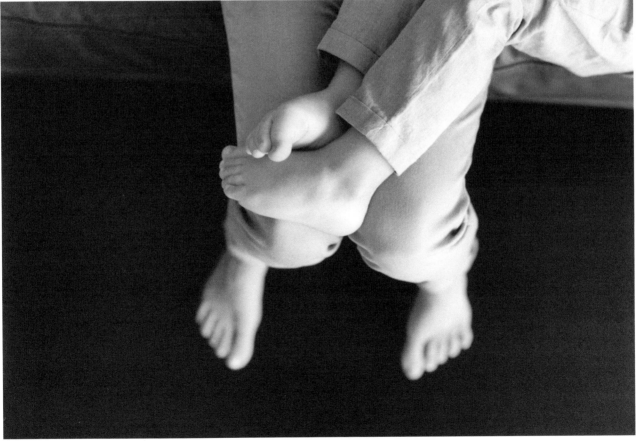

SHEEP TO SHAWL

The warmth of wool moves from one to another through a careful, methodical practice.

PHOTO ESSAY BY YOUNG & HUNGRY & STYLING BY EMMA ROBERTSON

SHEAR

DESIGN

KNIT

WEAR

INTERVIEW: ANY STYLE CATERING

INTERVIEW BY JESSICA COMINGORE & PHOTOGRAPHS BY MICHAEL MULLER

Collaborating in the kitchen can be a trying task, but Alice Crow and Ann Lowe of Any Style Catering have seemingly perfected the art of carving out their own unique roles within their two-woman business. Alice and Ann started cooking together to cater a friend's art opening, and the company was quickly born as a way to fulfill their shared love of food and desire to bring thoughtful, simple design into the dishes and experiences they create together.

Ann and Alice are based in Austin, Texas, where they take advantage of the thriving local movement of foodie culture that Austinites have embraced over the last decade. Their combined genius has graced many plates and tables over the past three years (including those of the Austin *Kinfolk* dinner), and while Ann and Alice both may have larger personal pursuits ahead beyond Any Style, there's no question they will both be sharing their creative culinary gifts with willing eaters for years to come. We sat down with Alice to hear a bit more about the inspiration and motivation behind their collective energy in the kitchen.

Where do you draw inspiration from, when coming up with recipes and creating your events? How do you ensure that the food and atmosphere complement each other? We draw inspiration, almost entirely, from the season. Not only does this influence flavor, but the atmosphere as well. In the summer when the heat is exhausting, we keep the flavors super simple (along with style) and let the color and flavor of the watermelons and tomatoes speak for themselves. In the winter, we love to braise. Dark, warm, and comforting are words that summarize not only the food, but the style we go with in the cold months. Having said this, we usually try to bring relief to these rich flavors by adding something crunchy or light in flavor, either in a course of its own or as a component of a dish.

How do you stay informed about local and seasonal produce—do you have a few favorite sources you rely on? We try to make it to the farmers' market every week to see what the local farms are peddling. Some weeks we overbuy and have a hard time cooking everything we've purchased, and sometimes we just go to look. Also, Ann manages a small grocery store in town, in which she chooses the local products/ produce she wants to carry. This has been a good way to stay in tune to what is being locally produced.

What are your must-have tools in the kitchen? A micro-plane, hand-held mandoline, a good peeler, a good strainer, and a sharp knife would be difficult to give up. I also recently invested in larger stand mixer, which makes a world of a difference in the baking/pastry portion of Any Style.

Do your personal aesthetic and lifestyle inform the way you approach cooking and event planning? One hundred percent. My own style has changed and grown immensely since I started catering and I could not be happier that it happened alongside Ann. She has one of the best styles and eyes for design that I have ever encountered, and I have learned so much from working with her. As for cooking and event planning, this is how I see it—we cook food and create events that we ourselves would want to eat and attend. So, if you know Ann or I, and you like our style and trust our taste, then chances are, you will like what we do.

Did you grow up in the kitchen with a passion for cooking—or was the discovery more recent? For me, the discovery was more recent. My mother is not a huge fan of being in the kitchen, so I really have no idea where my love came from. In high school, I got my first kitchen job in South Texas working for the dad of one of my best friends. I just kept going from there. Cooking in a few more kitchens, during and after college, led me to realize that I wanted to be making my own food on my own time. So, I did. ○○○

HOLIDAY VIGNETTES

A cherished holiday memory can act as a portrait of a person.

PHOTO ESSAY BY JOHN TROXEL

1. I love the elegance of figure skating, and it is my favorite winter Olympic sport.

AMBER GIBSON

---

2. My favorite holiday memory is when the family all comes together and we have a home-cooked meal. On Christmas Eve we get two ornaments from my parents every year. The tree can barely hold them all and slightly leans to the right.

BRYAN WHITELY

---

3. Stories, heirlooms, and culture are what bring families together and make the holidays truly memorable. Christmas Eve visits to my grandmother's were always filled with curiosity about the painted eggs and nesting dolls that decorated her mantel.

ALEX LANIOSZ

---

4. Sipping cider during the holidays is my perfect way to warm up the most blustery of days.

TAYLOR THORNTON

GREAT AUNT BETTY'S BREAD SAUCE

We also discovered the sting of a new tradition turning out to be a damp squib,
or indeed, a downright disaster.

OK, I'll be honest. When I was a kid, Christmas wasn't great. When a family is doing its best not to fly apart at the seams, taking the dogs for a rain-sodden drag around the block is as good as it gets. Christmas is all about family traditions, but when the dust settled and the jaggedy edges were smoothed over, we had to face the truth: we didn't *have* a Great Aunt Betty whose bread sauce had graced our table since time immemorial. All we had, alongside a certain lopsided charm, was my mother's conviction that *this* year was going to be special. So in the absence of genuine traditions, we set about inventing new ones.

We discovered the anticipation of lifting the lid from the proverbial pot and peering inside. Is this it? Is this the wonderful thing we'll do *every* year? We also discovered the sting of a new tradition turning out to be a damp squib, or indeed, a downright disaster. There was the year mum bought Christmas in a Box, ordered from a frozen food store catalogue. The minuscule cardboard carton landed on our doorstep the moment the shops shut for three days, and would have struggled to hold a fair-sized turkey breast, let alone Christmas dinner for mum, my two sisters, and me with all the treats and trimmings. Then there was the year that the younger of my two sisters decided to boost our Christmas cheer with Irish cream liqueur, Asti Spumante and sherry. Breakfast joy was followed by lunchtime queasiness. We pressed grimly on to a late, burnt dinner through fits of tired giggles. Another year, mum decided to make everyone their favorite food for dinner. There were six of us with my sisters' boyfriends in tow. She emerged after four hours, bedraggled by the formidable logistics,

only to discover that my mushroom soup and prawn curry had gone missing in action and my older sister's warmed-up cheeseburgers went against the laws of nature.

Some innovations did stick, however. My taking over cooking duty, from my very relieved mother, not only boosted our dietary fiber and vitamin intake by shielding us from her prodigious proclivity for frozen food, it also kicked off my life-long love affair with food. I swooned with delight amidst ten types of vegetable, wondering why no-one had alerted me thus far to the pleasures of the honey-roast parsnip. There was the tradition of Christmas in the country in a rented cottage. Early mobilization was a requisite, since the best ones get snapped up by Easter, but no one had to sofa-surf if our ranks were swollen by husbands and best friends, no one was left with all the washing up, and no one had to drive halfway across the country to get to their bed come nightfall. Instead, we revelled in post-breakfast walks through the snowy Welsh mountains and the gentle art of the jigsaw.

Now both my sisters are mothers, and where there were originally just the four of us, the family has grown to a very lucky thirteen. These days, we're cool with presents on the 27th if it's the in-laws' turn, and we understand that nothing is more important than making sure the kids don't spend all day in the car when they'd rather be home with their new toys. We've worked out that the best traditions are the ones you do year in, year out because you really want to, not because you always have.

WORDS BY RICHARD ASLAN & PHOTOGRAPH BY MARK WEINBERG

A BRIEF HISTORY OF BREAKFAST

This all-important meal has quite the storied past—and present.

Before there were forefathers and Stamp Acts and rebel tea parties in the local harbor, there were many uses for corn on the breakfast table. Breads, mush, cakes, porridge: the average early American cook was like a composer scoring a symphony with only one note available. There was no wheat then, at least not yet, and no coffee, juice, or tea; the cost of those exotic imports was not realistic for a small settlement on the other side of the ocean. Instead, the working man drank beer or hard cider, both beverages rich with fermented nutrients, before heading out into the new, unbroken fields.

Later, when people knew the land better, breakfast carried a more varied tune. Wheat was more available, and trade became easier as ship routes expanded. Fruits were grown and made into pies that could keep into the morning, a small miracle in the age before refrigeration. Animals were raised, meats cured, and salt pork, bacon's brother, could keep in the cellar for months.

The breakfast table grew modestly, a reflection of the earth's slow yield and a testament to the rigor of the Puritan lifestyle. In his memoirs, Benjamin Franklin recalled, "We kept no idle servants, our table was plain and simple, our furniture of the cheapest. For instance, my breakfast was a long time bread and milk (no tea), and I ate it out of a two-penny earthen porringer with a pewter spoon."[6] The unadorned table was a thing of pride, proof of a life too occupied with honest work for ornamentation.

As the country flourished, one change led to many more, and soon, a small settlement became a state. A union of them became a nation. In the south, breakfast was a grand affair, long and leisurely and late in the morning: biscuits and gravy, fried ham and oysters, even imported chocolate warmed with milk. Northerners, ever frugal, were appalled by this extravagance, but perhaps their appetites were more forgiving.

More people came and settled, and with them came their breakfast tables. The Swedes brought coffee cake. The Danish brought their pastries, the Austrians *strudel*, and the Dutch *oliebollen*. It was as if someone were hosting a party and had sent out invitations in a dozen languages, instructing everyone to bring something new to try.

And so it went, the steady rhythms of days and work. Bread and cheese and cold meats were eaten in the summer months for energy, and iced currants, slices of watermelon, and cantaloupe halves were enjoyed on golden, sultry mornings. In the winter, the fire kept the buckwheat cakes and baked pumpkin warm, foods prized for their comfort and heat.

Eventually, driven to offices and city centers, few people worked at home, fewer gathered at midday to eat, and the evening meal developed into a lavish event. Harriet Beecher Stowe wrote in a letter that a British gentleman, bored of the formal dinner fuss and nostalgic for the candidness of breakfast, felt that "You invite a man to dinner because you *must* invite him…but you invite a man to breakfast because you want to see *him*."[7]

Though breakfast continued to be dramatically transformed by industrialization, fit into cardboard boxes, and sold at stores—a long way from the porridge of corn that needed hours of tending—some things remain the same: we still gather in the most intimate hours of the day to make plans and to fortify each other, both in sustenance and society. We still share the foods and traditions that make up a part of who we are and where we've been, be it on a ship that traveled across the ocean or the one in the dream we just woke from. We still come to the table like pilgrims, wanting a fresh start in the new world that is each day.

WORDS BY SARAH SUKSIRI & PHOTOGRAPH BY YOUNG & HUNGRY

BROOKLYN STOOP

A simple set of stairs, the entrance to a building, becomes more as it's shared and loved.

Before I moved to New York, I didn't know what a stoop was. My introduction came recently, when my boyfriend moved into a renovated pre-war brownstone in Brooklyn. I walked up the steps, surveyed the meager shreds of green still alive within a jumble of pots, and hurriedly closed the door behind me.

Several weeks later, his roommate organized a stoop party on the steps. We joined in, cautiously. Somehow, the idea of getting to know the rest of the building's residents seemed foreign. Up until that moment, I'd lived in the same apartment for two years without ever crossing paths with my upstairs neighbor.

The party, small affair that it was, marked a clear before and after. Here's why. When you live in a place where space is viewed as a commodity, a luxury even, you become greedy about it. You clutch it close, and maybe only invite in those dearest. Stoop life challenges that notion. You are living in the open. Without a hedge to block out inquisitive eyes. Without a wall to buffer the whine of the ice-cream truck. In the simplest of ways, you are forced to relearn the art of sharing.

Over time, the stoop has become our outdoor living room. Those stains, scuff marks, and odds and ends that created the backstory of the building now feed into my story. The Italian espresso can, a makeshift cigarette holder, that has prompted many a smoke break and an excuse for a beer on the steps. The assortment of gardening tools jumbled in the entryway corner that heralds the beautification process of the stoop's plant life. The spatter of dark spots on the third step, left over from a particularly delicious slice of Neapolitan-style pizza. The small plastic water bowl, hidden behind a planter, that signals that this stoop has been adopted by a neighborhood Siamese, still unnamed.

The trail of crumbs, both figurative and real, has become a clue about the comings and goings of the residents at 371A. They are frequent patrons of the local *taqueria*. A green thumb in the building is sorely needed. As is a broom. But mostly, they are happy and easy-going. They are lucky to have each other as neighbors.

I don't even live in the building, but I see how the stoop has brought them together. Somehow, it changes things. Just like it did for the cat.

WORDS BY RACHEL BROWN

PHOTOGRAPH BY RACHEL BROWN & ADAM JONES

LOOSE-LEAF BOOKENDS

A small but special ritual begins and ends each day for a mindful couple.

It started with a shared pot of tea. My wife and I have now settled into a routine that we've come to refer to as our "daily bookends." The key ingredients include carefully chosen loose-leaf teas and a deliberate attempt to do very little. The premise is simple: each day begins and ends with a thoughtfully prepared, and slowly consumed, cup of tea. The ceremonial rituals create our morning and evening bookends, serving as small windows of daily clarity and peacefulness. As part of the ritual, the tea is attentively prepared, always a comfortable distance from the day's pending (and preceding) obligations. Quite noticeably, the morning and evening bookends each bring distinctive nuances that are experienced and enjoyed in different ways.

The morning tea, and our ensuing conversation, is meant to invigorate us and to serve as an anchor to help secure our footing for what the day will soon reveal. We typically chose a black tea from a small—but growing—repertoire of teas from near and far. A British breakfast variety has been our "go-to" as of late, enjoyed in thick mugs, sometimes with a splash of milk and a pinch of brown sugar (metaphors for armor shielding us from any trouble that may cross our path throughout the day ahead). We raise our mugs with a toast and take a few sips before settling into a review of our aspirations—remaining careful not to lose our connectiveness,

and taking in the peace and stillness of the morning. Streaks of sunlight materialize across the wooden table and the kids awake as we transition into the second cup. Oatmeal and fruit then join the equation, along with the buzz of domestic mornings.

I choose to bypass the coffee machine at the office, and instead make a variety of teas throughout the day. However, these are consumed in a different fashion. Each sip serves as a prelude to the evening bookend, which will be enjoyed in the absence of the wheels of commerce and the day's churning deadlines and demands.

The evening tea is meant to be uncomplicated. Moroccan mint is a favorite, with the steeped tea leaves representing remnants of a day well spent. All else is left behind, and hand-painted, cast-iron teacups are our reward for the accomplishment of getting our three children (all under the age of ten) settled down and tucked in for the evening—no small feat. The house settles, and a candle illuminates the same tabletop that, hours ago, served as the canvas for streaks of light from the awakening sun.

These morning and evening loose-leaf bookends connect us to the here and now, to each other, and to ourselves. They help bring a calmness and quietness to our otherwise noisy lives. They have become rituals for being present and more attentive.

WORDS BY SCOTT ANDERSON & PHOTOGRAPH BY RYAN ROBERT MILLER

BUVETTE: REFRESHMENTS

*Chef Jody Williams draws on her extensive travels, varied experience,
and collection of treasures to create a favorite New York venue for everything
from "newspaper to cork popping."*

INTERVIEW BY EVAN HANLON & PHOTOGRAPHS BY ALPHA SMOOT

monday - friday
8h00am - 2h00am

PINOT NOIR 16/58
CHARDONNAY
14/49
BARBERA D'ALBA
14/46
CDR
12/42
CHIANTI
16/52
BAUX DE PROVENCE
11/36
HI
13

The word "*buvette*," translated from French, means a host of roughly similar but not-quite-the-same things. One can go with "coffee stall" or "refreshment room" or even "pump room." But at its essence, it means something both specific and conceptual at the same time: "refreshments." It's this specific and conceptual form with which Jody Williams has imbued her *gastroteque*.

'We serve from sunlight to candlelight. It's bright and cheery, and you have your space to spread out and read the paper. At nighttime, we pop some corks, it fills up, and you lose your space. Or rather, use your space, differently.'

Such malleability of space and time also translate to homey ambience, wholly appropriate and necessary for Buvette, which is located on the corner of Grove and Bleecker in the West Village, New York City—home to long-term residents and camera-laden tourists alike.

'It's your piazza, *your place to come and do this or that. And it functions well in this kind of neighborhood. We have a lot of people who come in daily and go straight through from newspaper to cork popping, and there are plenty of others that come in and out all day. We get a little bit of everybody: those regulars as well as tourists just walking around who find themselves in front and intrigued. We don't take reservations. It's very egalitarian. Everybody can get in if you're willing to wait just a bit. It's just show up, squeeze in, and eat and drink all day and night. And things here move quickly. You don't have to wait long to find your place, usually. Though you never know on any given day.'*

The universal sense of home comes from more than just the clientele. There is a reason people stop in, and keep coming back, which begins with Williams's own beginnings.

'It sort of makes sense that I began in a very traditional way to learn to cook, and I'm here in a very traditional but innovative place to eat and drink, and do business, too. When I finished college I studied history and literature and I decided, "Oh, I'm just going to learn to cook." I was in San Francisco at the time, and it was really a vibrant and interesting place for food. Chez Panisse was going on. There were the old-fashioned farmers' markets out at the train station, where you would just get crates of vegetables. So it was that kind of scene where I put my foot in the kitchen door as a steward, just cleaning up and setting the house to see if I liked it, and I did. So I thought, well, "I'll just move out to New York and knock on doors."'

New Yorkers have always taken for granted their place in the pantheon of fine dining, even more so with the rise of a new Northern California sensibility around the province of food. The chaos of creativity and borderline lawlessness of eighties New York, however, created a very different experience for not just artists, but burgeoning chefs, as well.

'I moved to New York after college and just started knocking on doors. It was wild. Cooks in those days were party animals. Restaurants had their own culture that matched what the rest of New York was like at the end of the eighties, when the meat market was still a meat market. I would just read the Village Voice, look for jobs, and show up at the door. Still, I always gravitated toward the best. You know, what did I have to lose? And I would fake it. I would work as hard as I could, and I would fake as much as I could, and learn as fast as I could. And probably be the worst cook in the kitchen. But I thrived in that environment and the physicality of cooking. It comes to me innately. I have an oven in the back of my head, so when I walk away from the kitchen, I can still see what's baking.'

Buvette feels completely of a place and time in the modern New York, but there is a distinctly Continental feel that runs throughout the establishment. That Old World feel is both purposefully and instinctively imported by Williams from her own collection of overseas experiences and materials.

'I learned enough that I could really call myself a cook in New York City. So I decided to go to Europe to explore, and set up some opportunities. I was planning to spend six months in a little village near Bologna. I ended up staying for three years. It was a very kismet experience, a lot of floating without any real purposeful direction. I said, "When the ivy grows to the second floor, I'll move to Rome." And three years later, the ivy grew, and I moved to Rome. Once I got there, I said "If I just stay awake for three days, I can get a job, find a place to stay, and arrange my life here." And I did. I worked all over Rome. The Hassler at the top of the Piazza di Spagna, Harry's Bar on Via Veneto.'

The sojourn, however, did not end in Europe.

'I actually ended up in Japan, which was incredible. You see that Japan does French food like the French. I've had some of the best French wines in Japan. They get the culture, and that's what finally sunk in there. I was learning food, I was learning language, and ultimately I was learning culture. They're all so related that you can't really understand one without the other. Part of learning how to cook, you're learning how to live well. I got that especially in Europe. It wasn't about cooking, or the job, or learning how to be a chef. It's about life.'

After being out of the United States for six years and nearly as many cuisines, it was time for Williams to come home and start something for herself.

'One of the things about being self-taught is that you take the job to educate yourself and to risk, to learn, to put yourself out there. When that job doesn't fulfill those criteria anymore, that's it. I wasn't interested in just a paycheck, so I'd look for the next place, whether it was in pastry or butchery or a larger, more corporate organization. Eventually I got to a point where I had nothing to lose in starting to do my own thing.'

Buvette, however, is not necessarily a discrete form that was arrived at by a carefully articulated plan. If anything, it reflects the accumulative processes on which Williams has built her career, and more broadly, her life.

'I had ideas for a long time, and I'd accumulate them from all the corners of Rome while I was there. But it was only when I got back here that I realized I needed to start something that would bring all those things that I was missing together. I wanted to make a place where I would hang out, where friends would come together. If that meant sitting on wine boxes and cooking off a panini *press with an espresso machine, so be it, that's okay. That was the original idea. I wasn't planning a big restaurant. Let's just get a place we can fill. I've always worked in the Village, and so I started filling here.'*

And there's a whole lot of filling that's happened. Formerly the home of the Pink Tea Cup, Buvette retains the tin ceiling as a souvenir to its venerable precedent. The rest, however, is an externalization of the collection of experiences that Williams has gathered up until now: piles of corks, baskets of baskets, storied silver trays, and a seemingly endless supply of small plates and jars from which the *menu du jour* is served.

'It all started with writing a letter and making a phone call. I saw this space and said, maybe the landlord will speak to me. And he did. So we met, I told him what I wanted to do, and he said, yeah, let's build this place. Then you start getting the people together that you know can build what you want. Your tile guy, your painter, but most importantly, me with all my stuff. I've always had big collections of junk, dishes, silverware, boxes, antiques, and this and that. And slowly it's all found its way into the restaurant.'

Along with a large, hand-chalked outline of France, which looks out over the tile, wood, and slate dining room.

'I always wanted to do French. I had a great run of doing Italian, and I wanted to play with something else. I knew in my head there was a place called Buvette, and I just wanted to do it. I wanted to make tarte Tatin, *and* coq au vin. *I wanted to take big dishes and make them small, take an elaborate meal and make it in two bites. I wanted to work on a* gastroteque, *the American equivalent of a* vineria, *but that goes all day, so you can take your breakfast and coffee here, too. It can be your café, it can be your stand-up/sit-down dinner, your indoor/outdoor picnic. It can be all these neat things. You tell me what it is.'* ○○○

It can be your café, it can be your stand-up/sit-down dinner, your indoor/outdoor picnic.
It can be all these neat things. You tell me what it is.

—CHEF JODY WILLIAMS

MY WINTER GARDEN

When the days darken, soak up flowers indoors. Keep a vase on the table or some bulbs in your hand and the outside chill won't follow you home.

WORDS AND STYLING BY AMY MERRICK & PHOTOGRAPHS BY PARKER FITZGERALD

SETTING A SCENE and filling it with flowers is a simple way to keep spirits high. In a vase, on the wall, in a pot, or tucked in your hair or jacket—surrounding yourself with reminders of life wards off the winter blues. More so than any other season, winter needs flowers. A few poppies from Italy that are worth their weight in gold, or a blooming amaryllis picked up at the hardware store—every little bit lightens the load. Buy bunches, force bulbs, and repeat as necessary while looking forward. to the months to come.

From a bulb inside to a bud outdoors, winter fades.
Enjoy the subtlety, and watch for new growth.

Flowers always make people better, happier, and more helpful;
they are sunshine, food, and medicine for the soul.

BOTANIST LUTHER BURBANK[8]

SPECIAL THANKS

Paintings Katie Stratton

Art Director at Weldon Owen Ali Zeigler

Production Director at Weldon Owen
Chris Hemesath

WAYFARER

Photos 1 & 3 Nicole Franzen

Photos 2 & 4 Parker Fitzgerald

CRANBERRIES: BUSH TO BOWL

Cape Blanco Cranberry Farms

capeblancocranberries.com

Photo Assistant Jay Fitzgerald

MAKING A TRIBE

Tom McCready and Sleigh Bells Farm
and Gift Shop

EVERGREEN

Photo 1 Parker Fitzgerald

Photos 2–5 Leo Patrone

WINTER WEEKENDS

Wardrobe and Prop Stylist Lisa Moir

Food Stylist Katie Christ

Hair Rebecca Butz

Models Yolanda de Montijo, Frank Kofsuske,
Sasha Kofsuske, Ray de Montijo, Virginia de
Montijo

Assistant Robert Herrick

Props Brian Andriola, Alessandra Mortola

CLOSING PHOTOGRAPH

Leo Patrone

SHEEP TO SHAWL

Bearhill Farms

Art Boster & Kathy Gassen

bearhillfarms.com

BACK COVER QUOTE CREDIT

Rebecca Parker Payne for *Kinfolk*

ENDNOTES

1 Jack London, "To Build a Fire" in *The Call of the Wild and Selected Stories* (New York: Signet Classic, 1998), 147.

2 Margaret Visser, *The Rituals of Dinner: The Origins, Evolution, Eccentricities and Meaning of Table Manners* (Toronto: HarperCollins Canada, 2008), 45.

3 John Dewey quoted in: Lisa M. Heldke, "Recipes for Theory Making" in *Cooking, Eating, Thinking: Transformative Philosophies of Food*, ed. Deane W. Curtin and Lisa M. Heldke (Indiana University Press, 1992), 255.

4 Visser, *The Rituals of Dinner*, 99.

5 Marilynne Robinson, *When I was a Child I Read Books* (Toronto: HarperCollins Publishers, Ltd., 2012), 93.

6 Benjamin Franklin, *The Autobiography of Benjamin Franklin*, ed. Gordon S. Haight, Ph.D. (New York: Walter J. Black, 1941), 125.

7 Harriet Beecher Stowe, "Letter XIX," in *Sunny Memories of Foreign Lands*, vol. 2 (Boston: Phillips, Sampson, and Company: 1854), 7.

8 Luther Burbank quoted in: Effie Young Slusser, Mary Belle Williams, and Emma Burbank Beeson, *Stories of Luther Burbank and His Plant School*, ed. Lillian McLean Waldo (New York: Charles Scribner's Sons, 1920), 190.

**THANKS TO OUR
TORONTO DINNER PARTNERS**

Bellwoods Brewery

Coriander Girl

Domestic Curator

Fresh City Farms

Herriott Grace

HOI BO Studio

Kipos

La Merceria

Melinda Josie

Mjölk

Silverplate Press

Soma Chocolatemaker

Steven Alan

Stoney Lake Baking Co.

West Elm

Whole Foods

Your Time Boutique

WWW.KINFOLKMAG.COM

KEEP IN TOUCH